DIBELS™

Dynamic Indicators of Basic Early Literacy Skills™ 6th Edition

Administration and Scoring Guide

Overview
by Louisa C. Moats

Roland H. Good III • Ruth A. Kaminski
University of Oregon

DIBELS Oral Reading Fluency														
DIBELS Retell Fluency														
DIBELS Nonsense Word Fluency														
DIBELS Phoneme Segmentation Fluency														
DIBELS Letter Naming Fluency														
Initial Sound Fluency														
DIBELS Word Use Fluency														
End	Beg	Mid	End	Beg	Mid	End	Beg	Mid	End	Beg	Mid	End
Preschool	Kindergarten			First Grade			Second Grade			Third Grade		

08 07 06   11 10 9

ISBN 1-57035-896-6

Printed in the United States of America

Published and Distributed by

SOPRIS
WEST™
EDUCATIONAL SERVICES

A Cambium Learning™ Company

4093 Specialty Place • Longmont, CO 80504 • (303) 651-2829
www.sopriswest.com

188ADMIN

Acknowledgments

Supported by

Early Childhood Research Institute on Measuring Growth and Development

U.S. Department of Education (H024360010)

Institute for the Development of Educational Achievement, University of Oregon

The authors acknowledge with appreciation the assistance of Deb Simmons, Ed Kame'enui, John Bratten, Debby Laimon, Karen Rush, Mark Shinn, Michelle Shinn, Sylvia Smith, Ilsa Schwarz, Scott Baker, Shaheen Chowdri, Cheri Cornachione, Patricia Coyne, Shanna Davis, Kathleen Fleming, Jerry Gruba, Lisa Habedank Stewart, Beth Harn, Katherine Kohler, Elida Lopez, Dawn Sheldon-Johnson, Stephanie Vincent, Janet Otterstedt, Debbie Johnson, Ambre ReMillard, David VanLoo, Hank Fien, Diane Hill, Rachel Katz, Jennifer Knutson, Pamela Raya-Carlton, Catherine Doyle, Susan Stephani, Nancy Bank, Chantal Dufour-Martel, Jennifer Jeffrey, Katy Kimer, and Carol Stock

Letter Naming Fluency

Ruth A. Kaminski and Roland H. Good III

Based on previous research by Marston and Magnusson (1988). Supported by the U.S. Department of Education grant H023B90057.

Initial Sound Fluency

Roland H. Good III, Deborah Laimon, Ruth A. Kaminski, and Sylvia Smith

Based on *Onset Recognition Fluency* by Deborah Laimon and Roland Good. The authors acknowledge with appreciation the assistance of Melissa Finch, John Bratten, Nancy Bank, Ambre ReMillard, Diane Hill, Hank Fien, David VanLoo, Rachell Katz, Scott Baker, Stephanie Vincent, Lisa Habedank Stewart, and Marty Ikeda. Supported by a Student-Initiated Grant (90CD0819) funded by the U. S. Department of Education, Special Education Programs.

Phoneme Segmentation Fluency

Roland H. Good III, Ruth Kaminski, and Sylvia Smith

Based on a prior version of *Phoneme Segmentation Fluency* by Ruth Kaminski and Roland Good. The authors acknowledge with appreciation the assistance of Lisa Habedank, Dawn Sheldon Johnson, Scott Baker, Debby Laimon, Marty Ikeda, and others. Also supported by the U. S. Department of Education grant H023B90057.

Nonsense Word Fluency

Roland H. Good III and Ruth A. Kaminski

The authors acknowledge with appreciation the assistance of Sylvia Smith, Mary Gleason-Ricker, and Katherine Koehler.

DIBELS Oral Reading Fluency

Roland H. Good III, Ruth A. Kaminski, and Sheila Dill

Based on the work on curriculum-based measurement by Stan Deno and colleagues through the Institute for Research on Learning Disabilities, University of Minnesota. The authors acknowledge with appreciation the assistance of Sylvia Smith, Nancy Bank, Chantal Dufour-Martel, and Adeena Sarah and the data collectors.

Word Use Fluency

Roland H. Good III, Ruth A. Kaminski, and Sylvia Smith

The authors acknowledge with appreciation the assistance of Rachel Katz, Jennifer Jeffrey, Katy Kimer, Jennifer Knutson, and Carol Stock.

Dynamic Indicators of Basic Early Literacy Skills™ (DIBELS®) 6th Edition

Edited by
Roland H. Good III and Ruth A. Kaminski
University of Oregon

CONTENTS

An Overview of the Dynamic Indicators of Basic Early Literacy Skills (DIBELS)

What is DIBELS?

The Dynamic Indicators of Basic Early Literacy Skills (DIBELS) are brief but powerful measures of the critical skills that underlie early reading success. Supported by two decades of sophisticated research, these simple assessments predict how well children are likely to be doing in reading comprehension by the end of third grade and beyond. Three or four short tasks at each grade level, K–6, help teachers locate, monitor, and intervene with at-risk students in kindergarten through sixth grade. DIBELS assessment is a proven approach for taking "vital signs" of reading health.

Teachers or other personnel trained to administer the assessment give the screenings individually to all students in a grade within a short time frame. Screenings, called Benchmark Assessments, should occur three times per year.

- All students in a class are given the Benchmark Assessments three times per year.
- Only the at-risk students are given the progress-monitoring assessments.

DIBELS is based on the findings of two kinds of research: (a) research on the prediction of reading difficulty in young children; and (b) research on what is taking place in the minds of people who are learning to read. Scientists in many disciplines—cognitive psychology, neuropsychology, school psychology, language development, medicine and education—have achieved consensus on how children acquire reading skills, why some children have difficulty learning to read, and what kind of instruction is likely to help most children learn (National Reading Panel, 2000a). Each indicator in DIBELS measures a foundational skill whose contribution to reading comprehension is established (Rayner et al., 2001).

National concern over reading failure has been rising since the National Assessment of Educational Progress (NAEP) has consistently shown high rates of reading failure among fourth and eighth graders. In high poverty areas, up to 70% of minority children cannot read at even a "basic" level. In middle class communities, about 38 to 40% of students are failing to score at even a "basic" level in reading. They do not have even partial mastery of foundational reading skills and thus are not able to function at grade level or fully participate in their schooling. This reality is one of the primary causes of membership in the underclass in our society—the group for whom there are few opportunities for educational or economic advancement. The good news, however, is that reading is teachable if instruction is comprehensive, sufficiently intensive, and includes practices supported by research.

- Reading problems can be prevented in most children.
- Reading problems can be detected in kindergarten and early first grade.
- Children with problems do not spontaneously get over them; they need to be taught how to read!

The realization that reading skill is necessary for school success and that most reading problems can be prevented and ameliorated if they are caught early has driven many state and federal reading initiatives. Important research reviews (Armbruster, Lehr, & Osborn, 2001; National Reading Panel, 2000b; Rayner et al., 2001; Snow, Burns, & Griffin, 1998), policy statements (American Federation of Teachers, 1999; Learning First Alliance, 2000), and legislation (Reading Excellence Act, 1999; Public Law 107–110, 2001) promote early identification and intervention with students in the "basic" and "below basic" categories of reading achievement. DIBELS is a valuable tool for targeting instructional resources to those who need them most.

- The word "test" is less appropriate for DIBELS than "measure," "assessment," or "indicator" because DIBELS is a tool for planning instruction. It is designed not so much for determining a final outcome of instruction but to help improve those outcomes.

New state initiatives and those funded with Reading Excellence, Title 1, School Improvement, and Reading First funds require districts to demonstrate improvement with students at risk. End-of-year summative tests, such as the Stanford 9, Iowa Test of Basic Skills, Terra Nova, and Metropolitan Achievement Tests are often used in accountability systems designed to show overall progress. DIBELS scores are good predictors of performance on high-stakes, summative tests. Moreover, DIBELS is a tool that enables teachers to intervene with students at risk for failure before they take end-of-year assessments.

- DIBELS scores predict outcomes on end-of-year, high-stakes achievement tests.
- DIBELS scores help teachers group children for instruction.

The results of DIBELS can be used to sort children into groups for instruction tailored to their needs. The children's rate of progress can then be monitored on a week-to-week basis if necessary, and teachers can estimate how much more growth is necessary to bring students' reading to grade level. Reading "at grade level" means reading well enough to pass group-administered state tests of passage reading comprehension.

In the standards movement of the late 1990s, many states rewrote their literacy standards to enumerate component skills that must be mastered by students learning to read. Respecting current research on the nature of reading acquisition, many states included standards on both underlying or component reading skills, such as phonological awareness and reading fluency, and higher level comprehension skills, such as the ability to summarize a passage or evaluate an author's tone. Both component skills and the deployment of those skills for higher purposes are important to measure and both are highly interrelated. The "simple" skills measured by DIBELS, such as naming letters and segmenting speech sounds, predict reading comprehension so well that testing only needs to take 10 to 15 minutes per child and costs much less than more elaborate testing approaches.

- "Simple" tasks predict complex reading skills very well.
- Both foundational skills and comprehension will need to be taught.

Screening and Progress-Monitoring: Two Uses for DIBELS

DIBELS is a validated tool for early identification of children with potential problems and an assessment of response to instruction. The DIBELS assessment enables educators to modify their approach if a student is not on course to achieve district or state reading goals. Therefore, DIBELS fulfills two purposes: *screening* and *progress-monitoring*.

The *screening* function of DIBELS begins in kindergarten, even before students have learned to read words. It is carried out in the fall, mid-winter, and spring of each year through sixth grade. The *progress-monitoring* components of DIBELS are used selectively with the at-risk children on a week-to-week basis, if necessary, to determine how well they are progressing toward a goal. Again, the purpose of DIBELS is to catch the children at risk before failure sets in and to mobilize instructional support for them.

Summative tests given by districts and states reflect the end result of curriculum design, program implementation, and individual teachers' efforts over the course of an entire school year. The problem, of course, is that by the end of third or fourth grade when the summative tests are given, it is too late to plan and implement a more effective instructional program without considerable cost and effort. Intervention with older students takes much more time and is much more expensive and difficult to implement than early intervention (Torgesen et al., 2001). Schools can and should know how many students are likely to meet state standards far in advance of the spring date on which the high stakes tests are given.

- DIBELS benchmarks are used for screening and grouping children.
- DIBELS progress-monitoring is for tracking at-risk children's response to instruction.
- DIBELS may need to be supplemented with other diagnostic tests if students have suspected learning disabilities.
- DIBELS is not a summative or comprehensive evaluation of reading achievement.

Why Start Assessment So Early?

The road to reading success begins early in life. Early experiences with language stimulation, books, and the world outside home predict to a great extent how likely it is that a child will be a good reader. In addition, knowledge of letters, awareness of speech sounds in words (phoneme awareness), and the ability to link the two (the alphabetic principle) are prerequisites for early reading. These can be measured before the child actually learns to read. Even students with good preschool preparation are not immune to reading failure because reading demands linguistic and symbolic skills in which they may be weak. Moreover, those students with poor preparation for school in language, print awareness, or worldly experience will demonstrate signs of risk as soon as they enter school. Preschool programs such as Head Start are not enough to inoculate children against reading failure (Zigler & Styfco, 1994).

Thus, we need to do more than prepare children for school entry. We need to know how far they have progressed on the pathway to strong reading development so that we can intervene right away if they are falling behind the research-based benchmarks for growth. If we help students early, they are less likely to experience social, behavioral, or motivational problems that often accompany reading difficulty (Good, Simmons, & Kame'enui, 2001).

- DIBELS measures critical foundations for reading that can be directly taught.
- We can catch children before they fail and intervene successfully; children should not have to fail before they come to our attention and receive preventive instruction.
- Assessment in upper grades (4–6) can help us verify that our students are on track in the areas of fluency and comprehension.

Advantages of DIBELS

DIBELS was developed to meet these criteria:

1. *Scores are reliable.* DIBELS developers have been careful to define the conditions of standardized administration and careful to document the reliability of the individual measures. Thus, a child's scores are likely to be truly representative of their abilities. Retesting is easy if a child's scores seem unrepresentative of what they can do.

2. *Administration is economical and efficient.* The Benchmarks and progress-monitoring tests are relatively simple to learn, administer, and score, and the materials are less costly than similar instruments.

3. *Computer-based scoring system can track data on individuals and groups.* The University of Oregon maintains a Web site on which data can be entered, records kept, and results analyzed. This costs $1.00 per child at present (2004).

4. *Repeated assessment is possible.* The benchmark tests given three times per year use different items in each subtest so there is no practice effect from taking the test several times. The progress-monitoring tools have up to 20 different "probes" or tasks that are equivalent in difficulty. A child does not repeat the same task, although testing may be frequent with alternate forms.

5. *Subtest content measures foundational reading skills established by research.* Letter knowledge, letter-sound association, phoneme awareness, syllable decoding (non-word decoding efficiency), passage reading fluency, and passage retelling are all measured directly.

6. *DIBELS scores predict success or failure on a high-stakes criterion.* Low scores on DIBELS indicate the likelihood of failure on end-of-year achievement tests; high scores indicate the likelihood of success.

7. *Subtest scores are sensitive to small gains.* The effects of good instruction (designed according to research-based principles and components) are measurable even after short intervals.

8. *Instructional goals are given for each grade and skill.* Because of extensive validation research, levels of performance on foundation reading skills can be recommended and serve as "targets" at each grade level.

9. *Decision making about individuals is supported.* DIBELS identifies who needs help, what goals should be attained as a consequence of the instruction given, and whether the instruction is being effective week to week.

10. *Decision making about school systems is supported.* Data from groups of at-risk individuals can be used to determine whether the instructional support system and curriculum are leading to improvement, year to year.

- Reliability and validity are established.
- Tests are efficient and economical.
- Scoring interpretation and record-keeping can be done by computer.
- Repeated assessments do not spoil the results.
- Subtest content is research-supported.
- End-of-year achievement is predicted by DIBELS score.
- Instructional goals for each grade are established.
- Decision making for individual children is facilitated.
- Decision making around programs and curriculum is possible.

Finding the Research Base on DIBELS

The Early Childhood Research Institute on Measuring Growth and Development (ECRI-MGD) at the University of Oregon has constructed DIBELS, validated its ability to predict outcomes, and tested its reliability using data from thousands of young children in many regions of the country. The most current technical report summarizing the extensive research behind DIBELS is available from the University of Oregon (Good et al., in press).

Content of Measures: What and Why

The foundational skills that are causally related to complex reading behavior are now well established in a large body of scientific work that has accumulated over more than thirty years from many disciplines. DIBELS is designed to sample those skills and to direct educators toward teaching those skills. Additional *diagnostic* evaluation, such as that given by a learning specialist, language specialist, or psychologist, may be needed in areas where students are not making sufficient gains.

Benchmark assessments are given three times a year to all children in a grade. *Progress-monitoring* assessments are used electively when children's response to intervention needs to be closely followed.

1. Initial Sound Fluency (Kindergarten)

    Once called Onset Recognition Fluency, this subtest measures the child's ability to identify, isolate, and pronounce the first sound of an orally presented word. The examiner produces a sound and the child must find which of four pictures begins with that sound. For example, the examiner says, *This is a sink, cat, gloves, and hat. Which picture begins with /s/?* The child is also asked to orally produce the beginning sound for an orally presented word that matches one of the given pictures. The child's response time is measured by the examiner. The score is the number of correct initial sounds given per minute. The subtest takes about three minutes to administer. There is a separate collection of 20 alternate forms for progress-monitoring.

2. Letter Naming Fluency (Kindergarten to Grade 1)

    This subtest is a powerful indicator of risk for reading failure. Students are asked to name as many letters as they can, uppercase and lowercase randomly mixed, within one minute. The lowest 20% in a district are at high risk for failing to achieve literacy benchmarks, whereas the group between the 20th and 40th percentiles are at some risk. Long-term outcomes are greatly affected by instruction and learning opportunities.

3. Phoneme Segmentation Fluency (Mid-Kindergarten to End Grade 1)

    PSF is a direct measure of phoneme awareness. By the end of kindergarten, most children can take apart and pronounce the sounds of a three-phoneme syllable. Those who cannot may be exhibiting phonological processing difficulties, a warning sign for reading difficulty. The examiner gives the child a word or syllable with three or four phonemes and asks the child to say the individual sounds that make up the word. For example, the examiner says *sat* and the child says /s/ /a/ /t/. The score is the number of correct phonemes produced in one minute. The measure takes about two minutes to administer and has 20 alternate forms for monitoring progress.

4. Nonsense Word Fluency (Mid-Kindergarten through Beginning Grade 2)

    NWF measures the ability to link letters with sounds (the alphabetic principle) and use that knowledge to decode three-letter syllables that alone are nonsense words (sis, sil, com). The child reads randomly ordered VC (ov, ap) and CVC (sis, pom, ruv) words. The child receives credit for pronouncing individual sounds or the correct sounds in a whole syllable read as a unit. For example, the child receives three points for reading "raj" as a syllable or for saying /r/ /a/ /j/. All the vowels in the syllables are short vowels.

    The score is the number of letter-sounds correct in one minute. The child who reads whole syllables will receive a higher score because the rate of correct sound production will be higher than the child who pronounces each sound separately. The child who reads whole words is more fluent; his or her phonics skills are automatized to the point of useful application in word decoding.

    The subtest takes about two minutes to administer. There are more than 20 alternate forms for progress-monitoring.

5. Oral Reading Fluency (Mid-Grade 1 to Grade 6)

Benchmark passages at each grade level are used to measure accuracy and speed in oral reading of graded passages. A version of curriculum-based measurement of oral reading fluency was published as the Test of Oral Reading Fluency (Children's Educational Services, 1987a). The measure is used to identify children in need of additional assessment and intervention and to monitor reading progress.

Passages are calibrated for each level. Students read each of three passages aloud for one minute. The student's score is the median correct words per minute from the three passages. Errors are words omitted or substituted, or hesitations of more than three seconds. Immediate self-corrections are scored as accurate.

Twenty alternate forms of oral reading passages are available for progress-monitoring.

6. Retell Fluency (Mid-Grade 1 to Grade 6)

Designed as a check on comprehension of the passage read orally, this part of the oral reading fluency assessment asks children to tell as much as they can about what they just read. The score is the number of words the child uses to retell the story within one minute. Only words that illustrate the child's understanding of the passage are scored. (Irrelevant remarks or exclamations are not scored).

Children typically use about half the number of words in their retelling that they were able to read aloud in a one-minute timed passage. Thus, a child who reads 60 w.p.m. would typically use about 30 words to retell the passage. If children use less than 25% of the number of words read per minute (in this case, 15 words or fewer), there may be a specific comprehension or expressive language concern that merits further assessment.

Knowing they will need to retell the passage keeps children from thinking that oral reading fluency is simply for reading fast. The oral reading fluency score itself correlates very highly with comprehension, but the retelling adds authenticity to the assessment. Retelling correlates about .59 with the oral reading fluency score itself, indicating that it is a good additional check on students' attention to meaning.

7. Word Use Fluency (Fall of Kindergarten through Grade 3)

WUF is designed to assess vocabulary knowledge and expressive language for children at each grade level. The examiner says a word and asks the student to use the word in a sentence. The score is the number of words the child can use correctly in a phrase, sentence, or expression within one minute.

No benchmark goals are provided because the test is new and more data need to be gathered to establish its relationship with other measures of literacy. A general rule is that students who score below the 20th percentile are at risk for poor reading outcomes, and those between the 40th and 20th percentile are at some risk. Progress monitoring with

WUF is possible for grades K–3. Progress-monitoring assessments consist of 20 alternate forms at the same level of difficulty and are optional for students in the at-risk category.

DIBELS, By Grade and Time of Year							
	Initial Sound Fluency	Letter Naming Fluency	Phoneme Segmentation Fluency	Nonsense Word Fluency	Oral Reading Fluency	Retell Fluency	Word Use Fluency
K, Fall			▓	▓	▓	▓	
K, Winter					▓	▓	
K, Spring	▓				▓	▓	
K, ProgM		▓		▓	▓	▓	
1, Fall	▓				▓	▓	
1, Winter	▓						
1, Spring	▓						
1, ProgM	▓	▓	▓				
2, Fall	▓	▓					
2, Winter	▓	▓	▓				
2, Spring	▓	▓	▓				
2, ProgM	▓	▓	▓	▓			
3, Fall	▓	▓	▓	▓			
3, Winter	▓	▓	▓	▓			
3, Spring	▓	▓	▓	▓			
3, ProgM	▓	▓	▓	▓			
4, Fall	▓	▓	▓	▓			▓
4, Winter	▓	▓	▓	▓			▓
4, Spring	▓	▓	▓	▓			▓
4, ProgM	▓	▓	▓	▓			▓
5, Fall	▓	▓	▓	▓			▓
5, Winter	▓	▓	▓	▓			▓
5, Spring	▓	▓	▓	▓			▓
6, Fall	▓	▓	▓	▓			▓
6, Winter	▓	▓	▓	▓			▓
6, Spring	▓	▓	▓	▓			▓

How Do I Get Started?

If you are a kindergarten teacher . . .

- ❏ Read Administration and Scoring Guide.
- ❏ Have a stopwatch and clipboard.
- ❏ Attend workshop on administration; role-play and give practice tests with a team to ensure that scores will be accurate.
- ❏ Obtain Benchmark scoring booklet for each child in the class.
- ❏ Obtain two copies of student response material (one in reserve).
- ❏ Make an envelope or folder for each child in the class; children will be retested with the same Benchmark scoring booklet up to three times.
- ❏ Determine whether fall, winter, or spring assessments will be given. This depends on the *time of year*, not whether you are doing the assessments for the first, second, or third time.
- ❏ Arrange schedule to allow time to assess each child.
  - ○ Fall Benchmarks (ISF, LNF)   4 minutes/child
  - ○ Winter Benchmarks (ISF, LNF, PSF, NWF)   7 minutes/child
  - ○ Spring Benchmarks (LNF, PSF, NWF)   9 minutes/child
- ❏ Arrange booklets in alphabetical order to facilitate data entry.
- ❏ Check booklets against class roster.
- ❏ Test any students remaining.
- ❏ Enter data into the computer (http://dibels.uoregon.edu/).
- ❏ Obtain reports; file and/or distribute reports to appropriate personnel.
- ❏ Discuss results with grade-level team, coach, and/or administrator.
- ❏ Make instructional decisions.
- ❏ Use progress-monitoring assessments to graph progress of children at risk toward an established goal.

If you are a first grade teacher . . .

- ❏ Read Administration and Scoring Guide.
- ❏ Have a stopwatch and clipboard.
- ❏ Attend workshop on administration; role-play and give practice tests with a team to ensure that scores will be accurate.
- ❏ Obtain Benchmark scoring booklet for each child in the class.
- ❏ Obtain two copies of student response material (one in reserve).
- ❏ Make an envelope or folder for each child in the class; children will be retested with the same Benchmark scoring booklet up to three times.
- ❏ Determine whether fall, winter, or spring assessments will be given. This depends on the *time of year*, not whether you are doing the assessments for the first, second, or third time.

❑ Arrange schedule to allow time to assess each child.
  ○ Fall Benchmarks (LNF, PSF, NWF)   7 minutes/child
  ○ Winter Benchmarks (PSF, NWF, ORF)   9 minutes/child
  ○ Spring Benchmarks (NWF, ORF)   7 minutes/child
❑ Arrange booklets in alphabetical order to facilitate data entry.
❑ Check booklets against class roster.
❑ Test any students remaining.
❑ Enter data into the computer (http://dibels.uoregon.edu/).
❑ Obtain reports; file and/or distribute reports to appropriate personnel.
❑ Discuss results with grade-level team, coach, and/or administrator.
❑ Make instructional decisions.
❑ Use progress-monitoring assessments to graph progress of children at risk toward an established goal.

If you are a second, third, fourth, fifth, or sixth grade teacher …

❑ Read Administration and Scoring Guide.
❑ Have a stopwatch and clipboard.
❑ Attend workshop on administration; role-play and give practice tests with a team to ensure that scores will be accurate.
❑ Obtain Benchmark scoring booklet for each child in the class.
❑ Obtain two copies of student response material (one in reserve).
❑ Make an envelope or folder for each child in the class; children will be retested with the same Benchmark scoring booklet up to three times.
❑ Determine whether fall, winter, or spring assessments will be given. This depends on the *time of year*, not whether you are doing the assessments for the first, second, or third time.
❑ Arrange schedule to allow time to assess each child.
  ○ Fall Benchmarks (NWF [second grade only], ORF, RTF)   5 minutes/child
  ○ Winter Benchmarks (ORF, RTF)   5 minutes/child
  ○ Spring Benchmarks (ORF, RTF)   5 minutes/child
❑ Arrange booklets in alphabetical order to facilitate data entry.
❑ Check booklets against class roster.
❑ Test any students remaining.
❑ Enter data into the computer (http://dibels.uoregon.edu/).
❑ Obtain reports; file and/or distribute reports to appropriate personnel.
❑ Discuss results with grade-level team, coach, and/or administrator.
❑ Make instructional decisions.
❑ Use progress-monitoring assessments to graph progress of children at risk toward an established goal.

If you are coordinating schoolwide data collection . . .

❑ Schedule data collection about two weeks after major vacations or breaks. Plan around other major events on the school calendar.

❑ Decide on an approach to data collection.
  o In each teacher's class, teacher and assistant set aside 30 minutes per day for four days to test each child.
  o Schoolwide, a large team of trained people set up in a central location (library, cafeteria) and test all children in a day.
  o A core team of four to eight trained evaluators goes to each classroom and assists the teacher in collecting the data in one day.
  o Grade-level teams coordinate their schedules so that one teacher calls out and assesses her students while the class is visiting neighboring classes for instruction.

❑ Provide training for all data collectors.

❑ Ensure that data collectors have stopwatches, clipboards, and testing materials.

❑ Ensure that data collectors have role-played and practiced testing with team observers.

❑ Post data collection schedule at least a week ahead of time.

❑ Ensure that each student on each class roster has a booklet and data will be filed alphabetically in appropriate storage container.

❑ Contract with University of Oregon for data analysis and reporting (http://dibels.uoregon.edu/).

❑ Determine who will enter the data after testing is completed.

❑ Have extra materials available on day of testing.

❑ Remind data collectors to score tests as they give them; do not leave scoring for later.

❑ Organize booklets alphabetically by classroom; check against class roster.

❑ Enter data into the computer. (http://dibels.uoregon.edu/).

❑ File student testing booklets for future use.

❑ Obtain reports and set up meeting to discuss and present results.

❑ Distribute reports appropriately and file a master copy that will not be lost.

❑ Use data for instructional decision making.

❑ Determine who will be monitored with progress-monitoring tests; determine instructional goals and a schedule for checking children's progress.

Benchmark Expectations for Children's Progress

Benchmark goals and timelines for achieving them are summarized in the following table. These benchmarks have been established by research in different settings with thousands of children (Good et al., in press; Good, Simmons, & Kame'enui, 2001). The benchmarks represent *minimal* levels of satisfactory progress for the *lowest achieving* students (Good, Gruba, & Kaminski, 2001). One hundred percent of the students in the grade should achieve them if 100% of the students are to read at grade level or better. The benchmarks from grade to grade follow a progression in reading development wherein each step a child attains builds upon prior steps and is necessary for success in subsequent steps.

Time	DIBELS measure	Minimal goal for reading success	Cut-off for needing intensive support
Winter, K	Initial sound fluency	25–35 s.p.m.	Below 10
Spring, K	Phoneme segmentation fluency	35–45 s.p.m.	Below 10
Winter, 1st grade	Nonword reading fluency	50 w.p.m.	Below 30
Spring, 1st grade	Oral reading fluency	40 w.p.m.	Below 10
Spring, 2nd grade	Oral reading fluency	90 w.p.m.	Below 50
Spring, 3rd grade	Oral reading fluency	110 w.p.m.	Below 70
Spring, 4th grade	Oral reading fluency	118 w.p.m.	Below 92
Spring, 5th grade	Oral reading fluency	128 w.p.m.	Below 100
Spring, 6th grade	Oral reading fluency	135 w.p.m.	Below 110

Making Sure Scores are Accurate

Sometimes the benchmark test scores are inaccurate. Examiners make mistakes. Young children's test results may be unrepresentative of their actual performance because the children may be insecure, inattentive, unfamiliar with the requirements of the task, or just having a bad day. The advantage of DIBELS is that children can be easily rechecked if their group placement appears to be misjudged or the scores do not agree with one another.

The progress-monitoring booklets provide alternate testing forms that can be used to retest a child. By retesting a child on a different day or with a different examiner, we can be more confident that the scores are reliable. Two or three retests are usually enough to get a consistent picture of the child's actual level of skill.

Interpreting DIBELS Results

The intensity and type of instruction provided to children should match the degree of their difficulty. Again, the goal is to provide that help *before* reading failure becomes entrenched. The benchmark assessment identifies children who may need more intensive, slowly paced, or individually tailored instruction in order to meet the next benchmark. Highly effective regular classroom instruction that uses a research-validated comprehensive reading program will greatly reduce the number of children who need more intensive support. Those with emerging skills who are between the 20th and 40th percentiles can be taught effectively in small groups with programs strong on systematic, explicit instruction of foundational reading skills (letter recognition, phoneme awareness, letter-sound correspondence, phonic decoding, reading fluency). Such programs should also have strong components on vocabulary and language comprehension.

Children who score in the "deficit" or deficient range usually need one to one, or one to two expert instruction with a multisensory, systematic, structured language approach that attempts to rebuild a strong foundation for learning to read.

DIBELS Overview
© 2003 All Rights Reserved

Examples of Approaches Designed for Differentiated Instruction

Regular classroom, comprehensive core reading programs	Second-tier intervention, 20th–40th percentile	Third-tier intervention, below 20th percentile
Open Court (2002) (McGraw Hill)	*Read Well* (Sopris West)	*Road to the Code* (Brookes Pub.)
Harcourt Brace (2002)	*Early Reading Intervention* (Simmons & Kameenui), Scott Foresman	*Wilson Foundations* (Wilson Language)
Houghton Mifflin (2002)	*Project Read* (Language Circle, Bloomington, MN)	Lindamood-Bell
Reading Mastery (SRA)	*Reading Mastery* (SRA)	Alphabetic Phonics
Read Well (Sopris West)	Phono-Graphix	Orton-Gillingham
Scott Foresman	Spalding Approach	Slingerland
	WatchWord (Sopris West)	*Ladders to Literacy* (Brookes)
	PALS (Sopris West)	*Language!* (Sopris West)
	Sound Partners (Sopris West)	
	Colleague in the Classroom (Sopris West)	
	Six-Minute Solution (Sopris West)	
	Basic Skill Builders (Sopris West)	
	REWARDS (Sopris West)	
	Stepping Stones to Literacy (Sopris West)	

Teachers have many programs to choose from and will have additional well-designed programs as research on reading instruction continues and publishers improve their products to reflect the findings of research. Other variables that matter are the size of the group, the instructional time, the amount of appropriate practice, and emphasis on the skills most important for reading progress.

Specifying Instructional Goals

The plan for an individual student should specify goals that are steps to becoming a good reader. The goals should focus on essential skills (phonological skills, letter knowledge, sound-symbol association, word decoding, passage reading fluency, retell fluency). The plan should include the amount and type of instruction the student needs, the logistics of program implementation, and how progress will be evaluated.

For example, Brandon's plan (which appears on the following page) includes a goal for improvement in phoneme segmentation fluency and an "aim line" toward the goal.

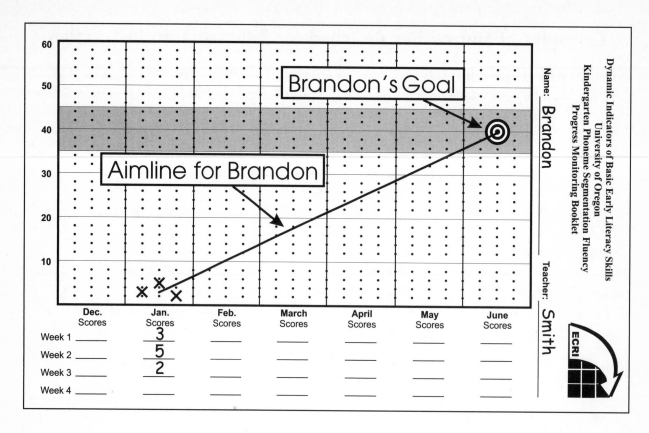

Evaluating and Using Progress-Monitoring Results

Interventions should be implemented with a progress-monitoring plan. If instruction is not having the desired effect, something should be changed to enable the child to progress more steadily toward the goal, if possible. In evaluating the effectiveness of an intervention, the following steps are recommended.

1. Decide how often progress-monitoring assessments will be given. The children with the greatest deficits should be assessed weekly. Others can be assessed every four to six weeks.

2. Establish a rule for deciding whether progress is satisfactory. For example, if three weekly assessments in a row indicate that the student is below the "aim line" of progress toward the goal, a change in approach is indicated. The instruction may need to target different skills, be more intensive, or use another type of instructional routine.

Schoolwide Decision Making With DIBELS

When regular classroom instruction is effective, about 20% of the children are still likely to need either small group or intensive instruction. If more than 20% of the children are failing to achieve benchmarks, then the program or its implementation probably need to be changed. The DIBELS Web site issues a report back to schools that answers the question: *What percent of students achieved essential reading outcomes?*

Below is an example of districtwide first grade reading outcomes for two successive academic years showing the distribution of scores on words read correct per minute on oral reading fluency (ORF).

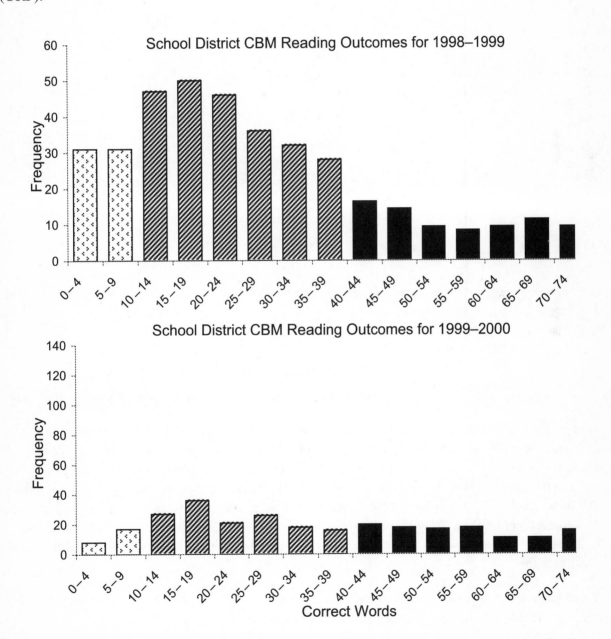

In addition, a "benchmark linkage" report shows how groups of children are progressing on the critical indicators of future reading success. Benchmark linkage shows the relationship between the students' achievement of earlier benchmark goals and their achievement of later benchmark goals. Below is a picture of the relationship between the achievement of initial sound fluency benchmarks (ISF) in a mid-kindergarten group and the achievement of phoneme segmentation fluency benchmarks (PSF) in spring of kindergarten for the same class.

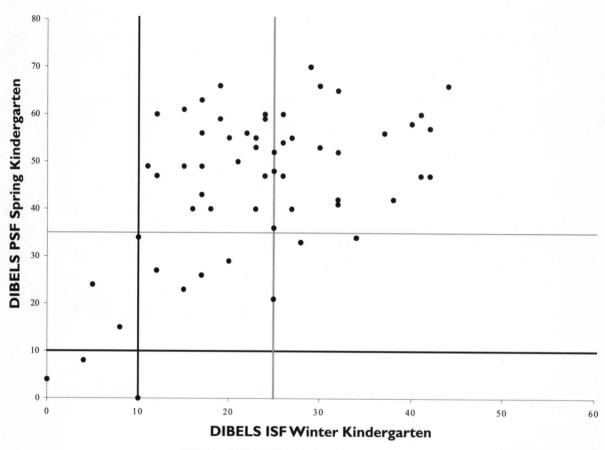

This graph shows that students who did not meet the earlier benchmark of initial sounds fluency in winter were also unlikely to meet the spring benchmarks on phoneme segmentation fluency. Students who were on track in identifying initial sounds in mid-kindergarten were then likely to learn to segment all of the sounds in spoken syllables. Twenty-seven students met the winter ISF benchmark of 25 or higher. These students are represented as dots to the right of the ISF 25 vertical line. Of these 27 students, 24 went on to achieve a benchmark score of 35 or higher in the spring PSF assessment. The number of dots shown above the horizontal line at PSF 35 illustrates this.

Three students in the class shown above remained severely deficient on both foundational skills and were candidates for intensive instruction beginning in first grade.

Benchmark linkage reports not only inform each teacher about the progress of each child but also inform administrators about the effectiveness of the school's curriculum. For example, a linkage report may show that students in a school began kindergarten with strong letter-naming skills, but because the instructional program did not include systematic teaching of individual speech sounds in words, students were no longer on course for achieving later reading goals by the end of kindergarten. Conversely, a linkage report can show that students began with a weakness on a benchmark, but because instruction was concentrated on accelerating progress, students actually gained ground in relation to the next benchmark.

In summary, linkage reports show that if more than the expected number of students are having trouble with a specific foundation skill, then the curriculum or its implementation may need to be changed. Not all changes will lead to improvements, however; such decisions should be informed by an understanding of reading psychology, reading development, and the theoretical underpinnings that link the major components of effective reading instruction.

The Role of Additional Diagnostic Testing

Students with reading disabilities are not all alike in their profile of strengths and weaknesses. Although the majority do have difficulty with phonological skills, others have primary or related difficulties with speed of word recognition. Many students with reading disabilities have coexisting and related problems with language comprehension or use. Their difficulties may extend specifically or globally to the processing of words, sentences, discourse, and pragmatics. Many have more difficulty with written expression than they do with reading. For all these reasons, additional diagnostic testing may be indicated so that intervention plans are based on a detailed understanding of all the factors that affect student learning.

Finally, surveys of students' knowledge of specific language concepts and associations may be needed to supplement DIBELS. For example, a phonics survey will inform the teacher about the sound-symbol associations the student has learned and which ones need to be taught or practiced. A spelling inventory tells which spelling conventions a student has learned along a progression of orthographic knowledge development. The Comprehensive Test of Phonological Processing (Pro-Ed) can round out the picture of phonological skill. A writing sample indicates how well a student can compose a narrative or expository text and how well the basic skills of transcription (handwriting, spelling, punctuation, organization of the work on the page) are developing. Additional language tests can help explain miscomprehensions of words, phrases, sentences, and discourse that affect listening, speaking, reading, and/or writing.

Technical Characteristics of DIBELS

A series of studies have investigated the reliability, predictive validity, concurrent validity, construct validity, and item sensitivity of DIBELS. Coefficients of reliability and validity can be found in Good, Gruba, and Kaminski (2001) and in Good et al. (in press).

DIBELS Letter Naming Fluency[1]

Directions for Administration and Scoring

Target Age Range

Letter Naming Fluency																				

Beg	Mid	End	Beg	Mid	End	Beg	Mid	End	Beg	Mid	End	Beg	Mid	End	Beg	Mid	End	Beg	Mid	End
Kindergarten			First Grade			Second Grade			Third Grade			Fourth Grade			Fifth Grade			Sixth Grade		

Letter Naming Fluency (LNF) is intended for most children from fall of kindergarten through fall of first grade. A benchmark goal is not provided for LNF because it does not correspond to a big idea of early literacy skills (phonological awareness, alphabetic principle, and accuracy and fluency with connected text) and does not appear to be essential to achieve reading outcomes. However, students in the lowest 20 percent of a school district using local norms should be considered at risk for poor reading outcomes, and those between the 20th percentile and 40th percentile should be considered at some risk. For students at risk, the primary instructional goals should be in phonological awareness, alphabetic principle, and accuracy and fluency with connected text.

Description

DIBELS Letter Naming Fluency (LNF) is a standardized, individually administered test that provides a measure of risk. Students are presented with a page of uppercase and lowercase letters arranged in a random order and are asked to name as many letters as they can. LNF is based on research by Marston and Magnusson (1988). Students are told that if they do not know a letter they will be told the letter. The student is allowed 1 minute to produce as many letter names as he/she can, and the score is the number of letters named correctly in 1 minute. Students are considered *at risk* for difficulty achieving early literacy benchmark goals if they perform in the lowest 20% of students in their district, that is, below the 20th percentile using local district norms. Students are considered at *some risk* if they perform between the 20th and 40th percentile using local norms. Students are considered at *low risk* if they perform above the 40th percentile using local norms. The one-month, alternate-form reliability of LNF is .88 in kindergarten (Good et al., in press). The median criterion-related validity of LNF with the Woodcock-Johnson Psycho-Educational Battery-Revised Readiness Cluster standard score is .70 in kindergarten

---

[1] Prior editions were supported, in part, by the Early Childhood Research Institute on Measuring Growth and Development (H180M10006) and a Student-Initiated Grant (H023B90057) funded by the U. S. Department of Education, Special Education Programs.

Kaminski, R. A., & Good, R. H. (2002). Letter Naming Fluency. In R. H. Good & R. A. Kaminski (Eds.), *Dynamic Indicators of Basic Early Literacy Skills* (6th ed.). Eugene, OR: Institute for the Development of Educational Achievement. Available: http://dibels.uoregon.edu/.

(Good et al., in press). The predictive validity of kindergarten LNF with first-grade Woodcock-Johnson Psycho-Educational Battery-Revised Reading Cluster standard score is .65, and .71 with first-grade Curriculum-Based Measurement (CBM) oral reading fluency (Good et al., in press).

Materials

Student copy of probe, examiner copy of probe, clipboard, stopwatch, and colored scoring pen.

Directions for Administration

1. Place the student copy of probe in front of the student.

2. Place the examiner probe on clipboard and position so that the student cannot see what you record.

3. Say these specific directions to the student:

   Here are some letters (point to the student probe). *Tell me the names of as many letters as you can. When I say, "Begin," start here* (point to first letter), *and go across the page* (point). *Point to each letter and tell me the name of that letter. If you come to a letter you don't know, I'll tell it to you. Put your finger on the first letter. Ready, begin.*

4. Start your stopwatch.

5. Follow along on the examiner probe. Put a slash (/) through letters named incorrectly (see scoring procedures).

6. If the student provides the letter sound rather than the letter name, say, *"Remember to tell me the letter name, not the sound it makes."* This prompt may be provided once during the administration. If the student continues providing letter sounds, mark each letter as incorrect and indicate what the student did at the bottom of the page.

7. At the end of *1 minute*, place a bracket ( ]) after the last letter named and say, *"Stop."*

Directions for Scoring

1. *Discontinue Rule.* If the student does not get any correct letter names within the first 10 letters (1 row), discontinue the task and record a score of zero (0).

2. *Three-Second Rule.* If the student hesitates for 3 seconds on a letter, score the letter incorrect, provide the correct letter, point to the next letter, and say *"What letter?"* This prompt may be repeated. For example, if the letters are "t L s" and the student says, "t" (3 seconds), prompt by saying, *"L.* (point to "s") *What letter?"*

Letters	Student Says	Prompt	Scoring Procedure
t L s U	"t" (3 sec.)	*"L. What letter?"* (point to "s")	t L̷ s U
i g W r	"i g" (3 sec.)	*"W. What letter?"* (point to "r")	i g W̷ r

3. *Self-Corrections.* If a student makes an error and corrects him or herself within *3 seconds*, write "SC" above the letter and do not count it as an error.

4. *Incorrect Letter.* A letter is incorrect if the student substitutes a different letter for the stimulus letter (e.g., "B" for "D").

Letters	Student Says	Scoring Procedure	Correct Letters
t D s U	"t…b…s…u"	t D̷ s U	**3**/4
t D s U	"t…d…g…o"	t D s̷ U̷	**2**/4

5. *Omissions.* A letter is incorrect if the student omits the letter.

Letters	Student Says	Scoring Procedure	Correct Letters
t D s U	"t…s…u"	t D̷ s U	**3**/4
t D s U	"t…u"	t D̷ s̷ U	**2**/4

6. *Similarly Shaped Font.* For some fonts, including Times, the uppercase letter "i," and the lowercase letter "L" are difficult or impossible to distinguish. A response of <u>either</u> "i" or "L" is scored as correct. For example, if the letters are "I (uppercase "i") D s l (lowercase "L")" and the student names them both L, score as correct.

Letters	Student Says	Scoring Procedure	Correct Letters
I D s l	"l…d…s…l"	I D s l	**4**/4

7. *Articulation and Dialect.* The student is not penalized for imperfect pronunciation due to dialect, articulation, or second-language interference. For example, if the student consistently says /th/ for /s/ and pronounces "thee" for "see" when naming the letter "C", he/she should be given credit for naming the letter correctly. This is a professional judgment and should be based on the student's responses and any prior knowledge of his/her speech patterns.

Letters	Student Says	Scoring Procedure	Correct Letters
c D s U	"thee…d…eth…u"	c D s U	**4**/4

8. *Skips Row.* If a student skips an entire row, draw a line through the row and do not count the row in scoring.

DIBELS Letter Naming Fluency
Assessment Integrity Checklist

Directions: As the observer, please observe setup and directions, time and score the test with the examiner, check examiner's accuracy in following procedures, and decide if examiner passes or needs more practice.

Fine	Needs Practice	√ box to indicate Fine or Needs Practice
❑	❑	1. Performs standardized directions verbatim: *Here are some letters. Tell me the names of as many letters as you can. When I say "Begin," start here, and go across the page. Point to each letter and tell me the name of that letter. If you come to a letter you don't know, I'll tell it to you. Put your finger on the first letter. Ready, begin.*
❑	❑	2. Holds clipboard and stopwatch so child cannot see what he/she records.
❑	❑	3. Starts stopwatch after saying "Begin."
❑	❑	4. At the end of 1 minute, places a bracket ( ]) after the last letter named and says, "Stop."
❑	❑	5. If child does not respond in 3 seconds, tells him/her the letter and scores the letter as incorrect.
❑	❑	6. Follows along on the examiner sheet and slashes incorrect letters.
❑	❑	7. Follows Discontinue Rule if child does not produce any correct letter names in the first 10 letters (one row). Records score of 0 for the probe.
❑	❑	8. If child says letter sounds instead of letter names, uses prompt, "Remember to tell me the letter name, not the sound it makes." Prompts once, scores further letter sounds as incorrect, and notes what child did on score sheet.
❑	❑	9. Records the total number of correct letter names in 1 minute.
❑	❑	10. Shadow score with the examiner. Is he/she within 2 points on the final score?

DIBELS Initial Sound Fluency[2]

Directions for Administration and Scoring

Target Age Range

Beg	Mid	End	Beg	Mid	End	Beg	Mid	End	Beg	Mid	End	Beg	Mid	End	Beg	Mid	End	Beg	Mid	End
Kindergarten			First Grade			Second Grade			Third Grade			Fourth Grade			Fifth Grade			Sixth Grade		

Initial Sound Fluency (ISF) is intended for most children from the last year of preschool through the middle of kindergarten. It may be appropriate for monitoring the progress of older children with very low skills in phonological awareness.

Description

DIBELS Initial Sound Fluency (ISF) is a standardized, individually administered measure of phonological awareness that assesses a child's ability to recognize and produce the initial sound in an orally presented word (Kaminski & Good, 1998; Laimon, 1994). The examiner presents four pictures to the child, names each picture, and then asks the child to identify (i.e., point to or say) the picture that begins with the sound produced orally by the examiner. For example, the examiner says, "This is sink, cat, gloves, and hat. Which picture begins with /s/?" and the student points to the correct picture. The child is also asked to orally produce the beginning sound for an orally presented word that matches one of the given pictures. The examiner calculates the amount of time taken to identify/produce the correct sound and converts the score into the number of onsets correct in a minute.

The ISF measure takes about 3 minutes to administer and has over 20 alternate forms to monitor progress. The ISF measure is a revision of the Onset Recognition Fluency (OnRF) measure incorporating minimal revisions. Alternate-form reliability of the OnRF measure is .72 in January of kindergarten (Good, et al., in press). By repeating the assessment four times, the resulting average is estimated to have a reliability of .91 (Nunnally, 1978). The concurrent, criterion-related validity of OnRF with DIBELS PSF is .48 in January of kindergarten and .36 with the Woodcock-Johnson Psycho-Educational Battery Readiness Cluster score (Good et al., in press). The predictive validity of OnRF with respect to spring-of-first-grade reading on CBM ORF is

[2] Prior editions were supported, in part, by the Early Childhood Research Institute on Measuring Growth and Development (H180M10006) funded by the U. S. Department of Education, Special Education Programs and Student-Initiated Grant (90CD0819) funded by the U. S. Department of Education, Special Education Programs. The authors acknowledge with appreciation the assistance of Melissa Finch, John Bratten, Nancy Bank, Ambre ReMillard, Diane Hill, Hank Fien, David VanLoo, Rachell Katz, Jennifer Knutson, Scott Baker, Stephanie Vincent, Lisa Habedank Stewart, and Marty Ikeda. Images are modified, published, and distributed by license from Nova Development Corporation (1998).

Good, R. H., Laimon, D., Kaminski, R. A., & Smith, S. (2002). Initial Sound Fluency. In R. H. Good & R. A. Kaminski (Eds.), *Dynamic Indicators of Basic Early Literacy Skills* (6th ed.). Eugene, OR: Institute for the Development of Educational Achievement. Available: http://dibels.uoregon.edu/.

.45, and .36 with the Woodcock-Johnson Psycho-Educational Battery Total Reading Cluster score (Good et al., in press). The benchmark goal is 25 to 35 initial sounds correct by the middle of kindergarten. Students scoring below 10 initial sounds correct in the middle of kindergarten may need intensive instructional support.

Materials

Examiner copy of probe, student practice pictures, student probe pictures, clipboard, stopwatch, and colored pen.

Directions for Administration

1. Place examiner copy of probe on clipboard and position so that student cannot see what you record.

2. Place the student copy of 4 practice pictures in front of the child.

3. Say these specific directions to the student:

    This is mouse, flowers, pillow, letters (point to each picture while saying its name). *Mouse* (point to mouse) *begins with the sound /m/. Listen, /m/, mouse. Which one begins with the sounds /fl/?*

CORRECT RESPONSE: Student points to flowers, you say	INCORRECT RESPONSE: If student gives any other response, you say
Good. Flowers begins with the sounds /fl/.	*Flowers* (point to flowers) *begins with the sounds /fl/. Listen, /fl/, flowers. Let's try it again. Which one begins with the sound /fl/?*

Pillow (point to pillow) *begins with the sound /p/. Listen, /p/, pillow. What sound does letters* (point to letters) *begin with?*

CORRECT RESPONSE: Student says /l/, you say	INCORRECT RESPONSE: If student gives any other response, you say
Good. Letters begins with the sound /l/.	*Letters* (point to letters) *begins with the sound /l/. Listen, /l/, letters. Let's try it again. What sound does letters* (point to letters) *begin with?*

Here are some more pictures. Listen carefully to the words.

4. Show the child the first page of student probe pictures. Point to each picture and say the name following the standardized directions.

5. Present the first question as written on the score sheet. After you finish asking the question, begin your stopwatch. Stop your stopwatch as soon as the child responds. If the child does not respond after *5 seconds*, score the question as zero and present the next question.

6. As soon as the student responds, present the next question promptly and clearly. Begin your stopwatch after you have said the question, and stop it as soon as the student responds, as above.

7. Score the child's response as either correct (1 point) or incorrect (0 points).

8. If the child stops or struggles with a question for *5 seconds*, score the question as zero and present the next question.

9. After the first 4 questions, proceed to the next page of student probe pictures. Continue until the end of the questions. When the child finishes the last question, record the total time on your stopwatch in seconds and add the number of correct responses. Record the total number correct and the time in seconds on the bottom of the scoring sheet.

10. Calculate the ISF Score using the formula:

$$ISF = \frac{60 \text{ x } Number\ Correct}{Seconds}$$

11. *Prompting Rule.* If a child has done the examples correctly and does not answer the questions correctly, say, "***Remember to tell me a picture that begins with the sound*** (repeat stimulus sound)." This prompt can be given once.

Directions for Scoring

1. *Discontinue Rule.* If a child has a score of 0 on the first five questions, discontinue the probe and give a score of zero (0).

2. If the child names the correct picture instead of pointing to it, score as correct.

PROMPT	STUDENT SAYS	SCORE
This is pie, letter, flower, and mouse.		
Which picture begins with /p/?	"pie"	0 ①

3. If the child renames a picture, and the *name begins with the correct (target) initial sound*, score as correct. For example, if the target picture is "hand" for /h/, and the student points at road and says "highway," score as correct.

PROMPT	STUDENT SAYS	SCORE
This is road, barn, hand, and egg.		
Which picture begins with /h/?	"highway"	0 ①

4. If the child renames the picture, and the *name begins with an incorrect initial sound*, score as incorrect. For example, if the target picture is "barn" for /b/, and the student points at barn but says, "house," score as incorrect.

PROMPT	STUDENT SAYS	SCORE
This is road, barn, hand, and egg.		
Which picture begins with /b/?	"house"	⓪ 1

5. *Correct Initial Consonant Sound.* If the word starts with an initial consonant sound, the child can respond with the first sound or initial sounds. For example, if the word is "clock," a correct initial sound would be /c/ or /cl/ or /klo/ but not /l/ or "clock."

PROMPT	STUDENT SAYS	SCORE
What sound does "clock" begin with?	/k/	0 ①
What sound does "clock" begin with?	/kl/	0 ①
What sound does "clock" begin with?	/klo/	0 ①
What sound does "clock" begin with?	/l/	⓪ 1
What sound does "clock" begin with?	"clock"	⓪ 1

6. *Correct Initial Vowel Sound.* If the word starts with an initial vowel sound, the child can respond with the initial vowel sound or initial sounds. For example, if the word is "elephant," a correct initial sound would be /e/ or /el/ or /ele/, but not the name of the letter /ea/.

PROMPT	STUDENT SAYS	SCORE
What sound does "elephant" begin with?	/e/	0 ①
What sound does "elephant" begin with?	/el/	0 ①
What sound does "elephant" begin with?	/ea/	⓪ 1
What sound does "elephant" begin with?	/ele/	0 ①

7. Schwa sound (/u/) added to a consonant is not counted as an error. Some phonemes cannot be pronounced correctly in isolation without a vowel, and some early learning of sounds *includes* the schwa.

PROMPT	STUDENT SAYS	SCORE
What sound does "clock" begin with?	/ku/	0 ①
What sound does "clock" begin with?	/klu/	0 ①

8. *Articulation Difficulty:* The student is not penalized for imperfect pronunciation due to dialect, articulation, or second-language interference. For example, the student responds /th/ when asked for the first sound in "sink." If the student *consistently* says /th/ for /s/, as in "thircle" for "circle," he or she should be given credit for a correct initial sound. This is a professional judgment and should be based on the student's responses and any prior knowledge of his/her speech patterns.

PROMPT	STUDENT SAYS	SCORE
What sound does "sink" begin with?	/th/	0 ①

Pronunciation Guide

Different regions of the country use different dialects of American English. These pronunciation examples may be modified or distinguished consistent with regional dialects and conventions. See the "Directions for Scoring" section for clarification.

Phoneme	Phoneme Example	Phoneme	Phoneme Example
/ai/	bait	/th/	thin
/ea/	bead	/TH/	then
/ie/	tie	/sh/	shed
/oa/	boat	/SH/	measure or beige
/oo/	food	/ch/	chin
/a/	bad	/j/	jam or edge
/e/	bed	/p/	pen
/i/	bid	/t/	tap
/o/	cod or law	/k/	can
/u/	bud and "a" in about	/b/	bat
/uu/	good	/d/	dad
/ow/	cow	/g/	gun or frog
/oi/	noise or point	/m/	man or jam
/ar/	(1 phoneme) car	/n/	nap
/ir/	(1 phoneme) bird	/ng/	sing
/or/	(1 phoneme) for	/f/	fat
/ai/ /r/	(2 phonemes) chair	/v/	van
/ea/ /r/	(2 phonemes) clear	/s/	sit
/oo/ /r/	(2 phonemes) tour	/z/	zoo
		/r/	rat or frog
		/l/	lap
		/w/	wet
		/h/	hot
		/y/	yell

DIBELS Initial Sound Fluency
Assessment Integrity Checklist

Directions: As the observer, please observe setup and directions, time and score the test with the examiner, check examiner's accuracy in following procedures, and decide if examiner passes or needs more practice.

Fine	Needs Practice	√ box to indicate Fine or Needs Practice
❑	❑	1. Performs standardized directions verbatim:

This is mouse, flowers, pillow, letters. Mouse begins with the sound /m/. Listen, /m/, mouse. Which one begins with the sound /fl/?

CORRECT RESPONSE	INCORRECT RESPONSE
Good. Flowers begins with the sound /fl/.	*Flowers begins with the sound /fl/ (point to flowers). Listen, /fl/, flowers. Let's try it again. Which one begins with the sound /fl/?*

Pillow begins with the sound /p/. Listen, /p/, pillow. What sound does letters begins with?

CORRECT RESPONSE	INCORRECT RESPONSE
Good. Letters begins with the sound /l/.	*Letters begins with the sound /l/. Listen, /l/, letters. Let's try it again. What sound does letters begin with?*

Fine	Needs Practice	
❑	❑	2. Responds to correct and incorrect responses as directed.
❑	❑	3. Holds clipboard and stopwatch so child cannot see what he/she records.
❑	❑	4. Starts the stopwatch immediately after presenting the question and stops the stopwatch as soon as child responds.
❑	❑	5. Points to each picture while saying its name.
❑	❑	6. Moves through pictures and questions promptly and clearly.
❑	❑	7. Marks correct responses as 1, incorrect responses as 0.
❑	❑	8. If child does not respond in 5 seconds, scores question as 0 and presents next question.
❑	❑	9. Follows Discontinue Rule if child has a score of 0 after first 5 questions. Records score of 0.
❑	❑	10. Uses correction procedure if child did examples correctly but does not answer correctly: *Remember to point/tell me a picture that begins with the sound* (stimulus sound).
❑	❑	11. Records the cumulative time from the stopwatch in seconds.
❑	❑	12. Records the number of correct responses.
❑	❑	13. Shadow score with the examiner. Is he/she within 1 point on the number of correct responses and within 2 seconds on the total time?
❑	❑	14. Calculates score correctly: $ISF = \dfrac{60 \times Number\ Correct}{Seconds}$

DIBELS Phoneme Segmentation Fluency[3]
Directions for Administration and Scoring

Target Age Range

Phoneme Segmentation Fluency																				
Beg	Mid	End	Beg	Mid	End	Beg	Mid	End	Beg	Mid	End	Beg	Mid	End	Beg	Mid	End	Beg	Mid	End
Kindergarten			First Grade			Second Grade			Third Grade			Fourth Grade			Fifth Grade			Sixth Grade		

Phoneme Segmentation Fluency is intended for most children from winter of kindergarten through spring of first grade. It may be appropriate for monitoring the progress of older children with low skills in phonological awareness.

Description

DIBELS Phoneme Segmentation Fluency (PSF) is a standardized, individually administered test of phonological awareness (Good et al., 2001). The PSF measure assesses a student's ability to segment three- and four-phoneme words into their individual phonemes fluently. The PSF measure has been found to be a good predictor of later reading achievement (Kaminski & Good, 1996). The PSF task is administered by the examiner orally presenting words of three to four phonemes. It requires the student to produce verbally the individual phonemes for each word. For example, the examiner says, "sat," and the student says, "/s/ /a/ /t/" to receive three possible points for the word. After the student responds, the examiner presents the next word, and the number of correct phonemes produced in 1 minute determines the final score. The PSF measure takes about 2 minutes to administer and has over 20 alternate forms for monitoring progress. The two-week, alternate-form reliability for the PSF measure is .88 (Kaminski & Good, 1996), and the one-month, alternate-form reliability is .79 in May of kindergarten (Good et al., in press). Concurrent, criterion validity of PSF is .54 with the Woodcock-Johnson Psycho-Educational Battery Readiness Cluster score in spring of kindergarten (Good et al., in press). The predictive validity of spring-of-kindergarten PSF with (a) winter-of-first-grade DIBELS NWF is .62, (b) spring-of-first-grade Woodcock-Johnson Psycho-Educational Battery Total Reading Cluster score is .68, and (c) spring-of-first-grade CBM ORF is .62 (Good et al., in press). The benchmark goal is 35 to 45 correct phonemes per minute in the spring of kindergarten and fall of first grade. Students scoring below 10 in the spring of kindergarten and fall of first grade may need intensive instructional support to achieve benchmark goals.

---

[3] Prior editions were supported, in part, by the Early Childhood Research Institute on Measuring Growth and Development (H180M10006) and a Student-Initiated Grant (H023B90057) funded by the U. S. Department of Education, Special Education Programs. The authors acknowledge with appreciation the assistance of Sylvia Smith, Lisa Habedank, Dawn Sheldon Johnson, Scott Baker, Debby Laimon, and Marty Ikeda.

Good, R. H., Kaminski, R. A., & Smith, S. (2002). Phoneme Segmentation Fluency. In R. H. Good & R. A. Kaminski (Eds.), *Dynamic Indicators of Basic Early Literacy Skills* (6th ed.). Eugene, OR: Institute for the Development of Educational Achievement. Available: http://dibels.uoregon.edu/.

Materials

Examiner probe, clipboard, stopwatch, and colored scoring pen.

Directions for Administration

1. Place examiner probe on clipboard and position so that student cannot see what you record.

2. Say these specific directions to the student:

    I am going to say a word. After I say it, you tell me all the sounds in the word. So, if I say, "sam," you would say /s/ /a/ /m/. Let's try one (one-second pause)*. Tell me the sounds in "mop."*

CORRECT RESPONSE:	INCORRECT RESPONSE:
If student says /m/ /o/ /p/, you say	If student gives any other response, you say
Very good. The sounds in "mop" are /m/ /o/ /p/.	*The sounds in "mop" are /m/ /o/ /p/. Your turn. Tell me the sounds in "mop."*

    OK. Here is your first word.

3. Give the student the first word and start your stopwatch. If the student does not say a sound segment after *3 seconds*, give him/her the second word and score the first word as zero (0) segments produced.

4. As the student says the sounds, mark the student response in the scoring column. Underline each different, correct sound segment produced. Put a slash (/) through sounds produced incorrectly.

5. As soon as the student is finished saying the sounds, present the next word promptly and clearly.

6. The maximum time for each sound segment is *3 seconds*. If the student does not provide the next sound segment within *3 seconds*, give the student the next word. If student provides the initial sound only, wait *3 seconds* for elaboration.

7. At the end of 1 minute, stop presenting words and scoring further responses. Add the number of sound segments produced correctly. Record the total number of sound segments produced correctly on the bottom of the scoring sheet.

Directions for Scoring

1. *Discontinue Rule.* If a student has not given any sound segments correctly in the first 5 words, discontinue the task and put a score of zero (0).

2. Underline the sound segments in the word that are correctly pronounced by the student. Students receive 1 point for each *different*, *correct part* of the word.

3. Put a slash (/) through segments pronounced incorrectly.

4. *Correct Segmentation.* A correct sound segment is any *different*, *correct part* of the word represented by sounds that correspond to the word part. For example, the sound /t/ is a correct sound segment of "trick," as are /tr/ and /tri/ (see rule 10, Incomplete Segmentation).

Word	Student Says	Scoring Procedure	Correct Segments
trick	"t...r...i...k"	/t/ /r/ /i/ /k/	**4** /4
cat	"k...a...t"	/k/ /a/ /t/	**3** /3

5. *Schwa Sounds.* Schwa sounds (/u/) added to consonants are not counted as errors. Some phonemes cannot be pronounced correctly in isolation without a vowel, and some early learning of sounds includes the schwa. For example, if the word is "trick," and the student says "tu...ru...i...ku," they would receive 4 of 4 points.

Word	Student Says	Scoring Procedure	Correct Segments
trick	"tu...ru...i...ku"	/t/ /r/ /i/ /k/	**4** /4
cat	"ku...a...tu"	/k/ /a/ /t/	**3** /3

6. *Additions.* Additions are not counted as errors if they are separated from the other sounds in the word. For example, if the word is "trick," and the student says "t...r...i...ck...s," they would receive 4 of 4 points.

Word	Student Says	Scoring Procedure	Correct Segments
trick	"t...r...i...ck...s"	/t/ /r/ /i/ /k/	**4** /4
cat	"s...c...a...t"	/k/ /a/ /t/	**3** /3

7. *Articulation and Dialect.* The student is not penalized for imperfect pronunciation due to dialect, articulation, or second-language interference. For example, if the student *consistently* says /th/ for /s/, and she says /r/ /e/ /th/ /t/ for "rest," she should be given credit for correct segmentation. This is a professional judgment and should be based on the student's responses and any prior knowledge of her speech patterns.

Word	Student Says	Scoring Procedure	Correct Segments
rest	"r...e...th...t"	/r/ /e/ /s/ /t/	**4** /4

8. *Sound Elongation.* The student may elongate the individual sounds and run them together as long as it is clear he or she is aware of each sound individually. For example, if the student says, "rrrrrreeeeessssstttt," with each phoneme held long enough to make it clear they know the sounds in the word, they would receive credit for 4 phonemes correct. This is a professional judgment and should be based on the student's responses and prior knowledge of the student's instruction. When in doubt, no credit is given.

Word	Student Says	Scoring Procedure	Correct Segments
rest	"rrrrrreeeeessssstttt"	/r/ /e/ /s/ /t/	**4** /4

9. *No Segmentation.* If the student repeats the entire word, no credit is given for any correct parts. For example, if the word is "trick," and the student says "trick," circle the word and give 0 points.

Word	Student Says	Scoring Procedure	Correct Segments
trick	"trick"	/t/ /r/ /i/ /k/	**0** /4
cat	"cat"	/k/ /a/ /t/	**0** /3

10. *Incomplete Segmentation.* The student is given credit for each correct sound segment, even if they have not segmented to the phoneme level. Use the underline to indicate the size of the sound segment. For example, if the word is "trick," and the student says "tr...ick," they would receive 2 of 4 points.

Word	Student Says	Scoring Procedure	Correct Segments
trick	"tr...ick"	/t/ /r/ /i/ /k/	**2** /4
cat	"c...at"	/k/ /a/ /t/	**2** /3

11. *Overlapping Segmentation.* The student receives credit for each *different, correct sound segment* of the word. Thus, if the word is "trick," and the student says "tri...ick," the student would receive 2 of 4 points because /tri/ and /ick/ are both different, correct sound segments of "trick."

Word	Student Says	Scoring Procedure	Correct Segments
trick	"tri...ick"	/t/ /r/ /i/ /k/	**2** /4
cat	"ca...a...at"	/k/ /a/ /t/	**3** /3

12. *Omissions.* The student does not receive credit for sound segments that are not produced. If the student provides the initial sound only, be sure to wait *3 seconds* for elaboration. For example, if the word is "trick," and the student says "tr," you must wait 3 seconds before presenting the next word.

Word	Student Says	Scoring Procedure	Correct Segments
trick	"tr…(3 seconds)"	/t/ /r/ /i/ /k/	**1**/4
cat	"c…t"	/k/ /a/ /t/	**2**/3

13. *Segment Mispronunciation.* The student does not receive credit for sound segments that are mispronounced. For example, if the word is "trick," and the student says "t…r…i…ks," they would receive no credit for /ks/ because there is no /ks/ sound segment in the word "trick."

Word	Student Says	Scoring Procedure	Correct Segments
trick	"t…r…i…ks"	/t/ /r/ /i/ /k̶s̶/	**3**/4
cat	"b…a…t"	/k̶/ /a/ /t/	**2**/3

Pronunciation Guide

Different regions of the country use different dialects of American English. These pronunciation examples may be modified or distinguished consistent with regional dialects and conventions. See the "Directions for Scoring" section for clarification.

Phoneme	Phoneme Example	Phoneme	Phoneme Example
/ai/	bait	/th/	thin
/ea/	bead	/TH/	then
/ie/	tie	/sh/	shed
/oa/	boat	/SH/	measure or beige
/oo/	food	/ch/	chin
/a/	bad	/j/	jam or edge
/e/	bed	/p/	pen
/i/	bid	/t/	tap
/o/	cod or law	/k/	can
/u/	bud and "a" in about	/b/	bat
/uu/	good	/d/	dad
/ow/	cow	/g/	gun or frog
/oi/	noise or point	/m/	man or jam
/ar/	(1 phoneme) car	/n/	nap
/ir/	(1 phoneme) bird	/ng/	sing
/or/	(1 phoneme) for	/f/	fat
/ai/ /r/	(2 phonemes) chair	/v/	van
/ea/ /r/	(2 phonemes) clear	/s/	sit
/oo/ /r/	(2 phonemes) tour	/z/	zoo
		/r/	rat or frog
		/l/	lap
		/w/	wet
		/h/	hot
		/y/	yell

DIBELS Phoneme Segmentation Fluency
Assessment Integrity Checklist

Directions: As the observer, please observe setup and directions, time and score the test with the examiner, check examiner's accuracy in following procedures, and decide if examiner passes or needs more practice.

Fine	Needs Practice	√ box to indicate Fine or Needs Practice
❏	❏	1. Performs standardized directions verbatim:

I am going to say a word. After I say it, you tell me all the sounds in the word. So, if I say, "sam," you would say /s/ /a/ /m/. Let's try one. Tell me the sounds in "mop."

CORRECT RESPONSE	INCORRECT RESPONSE
Very good. The sounds in "mop" are /m/ /o/ /p/.	*The sounds in "mop" are /m/ /o/ /p/. Your turn. Tell me the sounds in "mop."*

OK. Here is your first word.

Fine	Needs Practice	
❏	❏	2. Responds to correct and incorrect responses appropriately.
❏	❏	3. Holds clipboard and stopwatch so child cannot see what he/she records.
❏	❏	4. Presents the first word, then starts stopwatch.
❏	❏	5. Reads words from left to right.
❏	❏	6. Waits 3 seconds for child to produce sound segments. After 3 seconds, presents next word.
❏	❏	7. Underlines correct segments and slashes incorrect segments according to scoring rules.
❏	❏	8. Presents words promptly and clearly.
❏	❏	9. Follows Discontinue Rule: If child does not produce any correct segments in the first five words, stops and records score of 0.
❏	❏	10. Stops at the end of 1 minute and puts a bracket ( ]) at the 1-minute mark.
❏	❏	11. Records the total number of correctly produced phonemes in 1 minute.
❏	❏	12. Shadow score with the examiner. Is he/she within 2 points on the final score?

DIBELS Nonsense Word Fluency[4]

Directions for Administration and Scoring

Target Age Range

DIBELS Nonsense Word Fluency																				
Beg	Mid	End	Beg	Mid	End	Beg	Mid	End	Beg	Mid	End	Beg	Mid	End	Beg	Mid	End	Beg	Mid	End
Kindergarten			First Grade			Second Grade			Third Grade			Fourth Grade			Fifth Grade			Sixth Grade		

Nonsense Word Fluency is intended for most children from mid to end of kindergarten through the beginning of second grade. It may be appropriate for monitoring the progress of older children with low skills in letter-sound correspondence.

Description

DIBELS Nonsense Word Fluency (NWF) is a standardized, individually administered test of the alphabetic principle, including letter-sound correspondence and the ability to blend letters into words in which letters represent their most common sounds (Kaminski & Good, 1996). The student is presented an 8.5″ x 11″ sheet of paper with randomly ordered VC and CVC nonsense words (e.g., *sig, rav, ov*) and asked to produce verbally the individual letter sound of each letter or verbally produce, or read, the whole nonsense word. For example, if the stimulus word is "vaj" the student could say /v/ /a/ /j/ or say the word /vaj/ to obtain a total of three letter sounds correct. The student is allowed 1 minute to produce as many letter sounds as he/she can, and the final score is the number of letter sounds produced correctly in one minute. Because the measure is fluency based, students receive a higher score if they are phonologically recoding the word and receive a lower score if they are providing letter sounds in isolation. The NWF measure takes about 2 minutes to administer and has over 20 alternate forms for monitoring progress. The one-month, alternate-form reliability for NWF in January of first grade is .83 (Good et al., in press). The concurrent criterion-validity of DIBELS NWF with the Woodcock-Johnson Psycho-Educational Battery-Revised Readiness Cluster score is .36 in January and .59 in February of first grade (Good et al., in press). The predictive validity of DIBELS NWF in January of first grade with (a) CBM ORF in May of first grade is .82, (b) CBM ORF in May of second grade is .60, (c) Woodcock-Johnson Psycho-Educational Battery Total Reading Cluster score is .66 (Good et al., in press). The benchmark goal for Nonsense Word Fluency is 50 correct letter sounds per minute by mid first grade. Students scoring below 30 in mid first grade may need intensive instructional support to achieve first grade reading goals.

[4] Prior editions were supported, in part, by the Early Childhood Research Institute on Measuring Growth and Development (H180M10006) funded by the U. S. Department of Education, Special Education Programs. The authors acknowledge with appreciation the assistance of Sylvia Smith, Mary Gleason-Ricker, Katherine Koehler, and Janet Otterstedt.

Good, R. H., & Kaminski, R. A. (2002). Nonsense Word Fluency. In R. H. Good & R. A. Kaminski (Eds.), *Dynamic Indicators of Basic Early Literacy Skills* (6th ed.). Eugene, OR: Institute for the Development of Educational Achievement. Available: http://dibels.uoregon.edu/.

Materials

Practice items, student copy of probe, examiner copy of probe, clipboard, stopwatch, and colored scoring pen.

Directions for Administration

1. Place the practice items in front of the student.

2. Place the examiner probe on clipboard and position so that the student cannot see what you record.

3. Say these specific directions to the student:

   Look at this word (point to the first word on the practice probe). *It's a make-believe word. Watch me read the word: /s/ /i/ /m/, "sim"* (point to each letter then run your finger fast beneath the whole word). *I can say the sounds of the letters, /s/ /i/ /m/* (point to each letter), *or I can read the whole word, "sim"* (run your finger fast beneath the whole word).

   Your turn to read a make-believe word. Read this word the best you can (point to the word "lut"). *Make sure you say any sounds you know.*

CORRECT RESPONSE: If the child responds with "lut" or with all of the sounds, say	INCORRECT OR NO RESPONSE: If the child does not respond within *3 seconds* or responds incorrectly, say
That's right. The sounds are /l/ /u/ /t/ or "lut."	*Remember, you can say the sounds or you can say the whole word. Watch me: The sounds are /l/ /u/ /t/* (point to each letter) *or "lut"* (run your finger fast beneath the whole word). *Let's try again. Read this word the best you can* (point to the word "lut").

4. Place the student copy of the probe in front of the child.

   Here are some more make-believe words (point to the student probe). *Start here* (point to the first word) *and go across the page* (point across the page). *When I say, "Begin," read the words the best you can. Point to each letter and tell me the sound or read the whole word. Read the words the best you can. Put your finger on the first word. Ready, begin.*

5. Start your stopwatch.

DIBELS Nonsense Word Fluency

6. Follow along on the examiner copy of the probe and underline each letter sound the student provides correctly, either in isolation or read as a whole word. Put a slash (/) over each letter sound read incorrectly.

7. At the end of *1 minute*, place a bracket ( ]) after the last letter sound provided by the student and say, **"Stop."**

8. These directions can be shortened by beginning with Number 4 for repeated measurement when the student *clearly* understands the directions and procedure.

Directions for Scoring

1. *Discontinue Rule.* If the student does not get any sounds correct in words 1–5, discontinue the task and record a score of zero (0).

2. *Correct Letter Sounds.* Underline the *individual letters* for letter sounds produced correctly in isolation and score 1 point for each letter sound produced correctly. For example, if the stimulus word is "tob," and the student says /t/ /o/ /b/, the individual letters would be underlined with a score of 3.

Word	Student Says	Scoring Procedure	Correct Letter Sounds
tob	"t...o...b"	<u>t</u> <u>o</u> <u>b</u>	**3**/3
dos	"d...o...s"	<u>d</u> <u>o</u> <u>s</u>	**3**/3

3. *Correct Words.* Use a single underline under multiple letters for correct letter sounds blended together and give credit for each letter-sound correspondence produced correctly. For example, if the stimulus word is "tob," and the student says, "tob," one underline would be used with a score of 3.

Word	Student Says	Scoring Procedure	Correct Letter Sounds
tob	"tob"	<u>t o b</u>	**3**/3
dos	"d...os"	<u>d</u> <u>o s</u>	**3**/3

4. *Partially Correct Words.* If a word is partially correct, underline the corresponding letters for letter sounds produced correctly. Put a slash (/) through the letter if the corresponding letter sound is incorrect. For example, if the word is "tob," and the student says "toab" (with a long o), the letters "t" and "b" would be underlined, and the letter "o" would be slashed for a score of 2.

Word	Student Says	Scoring Procedure	Correct Letter Sounds
tob	"toab" (long o)	<u>t</u> ø̸ <u>b</u>	**2**/3
dos	"dot"	<u>d</u> <u>o</u> s̸	**2**/3

5. *Repeated Sounds.* Letter sounds given twice while sounding out the word are given credit only once. For example, if stimulus word is "tob," and the student says /t/ /o/ /ob/, the letter "o" and the letters "ob" are underlined. The student receives only 1 point for the letter sound "o" even though the correct sound was provided twice (a total of 3 for the entire word).

Word	Student Says	Scoring Procedure	Correct Letter Sounds
tob	"t…o…ob"	t o b	**3**/3
dos	"d…o…s…dos"	d o s	**3**/3

6. *Three-Second Rule (Sound by Sound).* If the student is providing individual letter sounds and hesitates for 3 seconds on a letter sound, score the letter sound incorrect, provide the correct letter sound, point to the next letter, and say "**What sound?**" This prompt may be repeated. For example, if stimulus word is "tob," and the student says /t/ (3 seconds), prompt by saying, "**/o/** (point to "b") **What sound?**"

Word	Student Says	Prompt	Scoring Procedure	Correct Letter Sounds
tob	"t" (3 sec.)	/o/ (point to "b") *What sound?*	t o̶ b	**1**/3
dos et	"d…o" (3 sec.)	/s/ (point to "e") *What sound?*	d o s̶ e t	**2**/5

7. *Three-Second Rule (Word by Word).* If the student is reading words and hesitates for 3 seconds on a word, score the word incorrect, provide the correct word, point to the next word, and say, "**What word**?" This prompt can be repeated. For example, if stimulus words are "tob dos et," and the student says "tob" (3 seconds), prompt by saying, "**dos** (point to "et") **What word?**"

Words	Student Says	Prompt	Scoring Procedure
tob dos et	"tob" (3 sec)	*"dos* (point to "et") *What word?"*	t o b d̶o̶s̶ e t
tuf kej ik	"tuf" (3 sec)	*"kej* (point to "ik") *What word?"*	t u f k̶e̶j̶ i k

8. *Sound Order (Sound by Sound).* Letter sounds produced in isolation but out of order are scored as correct. For example, if stimulus word is "tob," and the student points to and says /b/ /o/ /t/, all letters would be underlined, with a score of 3. The purpose of this rule is to give students credit as they are beginning to learn individual letter-sound correspondences.

Word	Student Says	Scoring Procedure	Correct Letter Sounds
tob	"b…o…t" (point correctly)	t o b	**3**/3
dos	"o…d…s" (point correctly)	d o s	**3**/3

9. *Sound Order (Word by Word).* Blended letter sounds must be correct and in the correct place (beginning, middle, end) to receive credit. For example, if stimulus word is "tob," and the student says "bot," only the "o" would be correct and in the correct place, for a score of 1.

Word	Student Says	Scoring Procedure	Correct Letter Sounds
tob	"bot"	t̸ o̲ b̸	**1**/3
ik	"ki"	i̸ k̸	**0**/2

10. Insertions. Insertions are not scored as incorrect. For example, if the stimulus word is "sim," and the student says "stim," the letters "s," "i," and "m" would be underlined and full credit would given for the word with no penalty for the insertion of /t/.

Word	Student Says	Scoring Procedure	Correct Letter Sounds
tob	"stob"	<u>t o b</u>	**3**/3
dos	"dots"	<u>d o s</u>	**3**/3

11. *Dialect and Articulation.* The student is not penalized for imperfect pronunciation due to dialect, articulation, or second-language inferences. This is a professional judgment and should be based on the student's responses and any prior knowledge of their speech patterns. For example, a student may regularly substitute /th/ for /s/. If the stimulus word is "sim," and the student says "thim," the letter "s" would be underlined and credit for a correct letter-sound correspondence would be given.

Word	Student Says	Scoring Procedure	Correct Letter Sounds
sim	"thim" (articulation error)	<u>s i m</u>	**3**/3
rit	"wit" (articulation error)	<u>r i t</u>	**3**/3

12. *Self-Corrections.* If a student makes an error and corrects himself within 3 seconds, write "SC" above the letter sound or word and count it as correct.

13. *Skips Row.* If a student skips an entire row, draw a line through the row and do not count the row in scoring.

Pronunciation Guide

Different regions of the country use different dialects of American English. These pronunciation examples may be modified or distinguished consistent with regional dialects and conventions. See the "Directions for Scoring" section for clarification. The letters "x" and "q" are not used. The letters "h," "w," "y," and "r" are used only in the initial position. The letters "c" and "g" are used only in the final position.

Letter	Sound	Example
a	/a/	bat
e	/e/	bet
i	/i/	bit
o	/o/	top
u	/u/	hut
b	/b/	bat
c	/k/	tic
d	/d/	dad
f	/f/	fan
g	/g/	pig
h	/h/	hat
j	/j/	jet
k	/k/	can
l	/l/	lot
m	/m/	man
n	/n/	not
p	/p/	pan
r	/r/	ran
s	/s/	sat
t	/t/	top
v	/v/	van
w	/w/	wet
y	/y/	yak
z	/z/	zipper

DIBELS Nonsense Word Fluency

DIBELS Nonsense Word Fluency
Assessment Integrity Checklist

Directions: As the observer, please observe setup and directions, time and score the test with the examiner, check examiner's accuracy in following procedures, and decide if examiner passes or needs more practice.

Fine	Needs Practice	√ box to indicate Fine or Needs Practice
❏	❏	1. Performs standardized directions verbatim:

Look at this word. It's a make-believe word. Watch me read the word: /s/ /i/ /m/, "sim." I can say the sounds of the letters, /s/ /i/ /m/, or I can read the whole word, "sim."

Your turn to read a make-believe word. Read this word the best you can (point to the word "lut"). Make sure you say any sounds you know.

CORRECT RESPONSE	INCORRECT RESPONSE
That's right. The sounds are /l/ /u/ /t/ or "lut."	*Remember, you can say the sounds or you can say the whole word. Watch me: The sounds are /l/ /u/ /t/ or "lut." Lets try again. Read this word the best you can.*

Here are some more make-believe words. Start here and go across the page. When I say, "Begin," read the words the best you can. Point to each letter and tell me the sound or read the whole word. Read the words the best you can. Put your finger on the first word. Ready, begin.

Fine	Needs Practice	
❏	❏	2. Responds to correct and incorrect responses appropriately.
❏	❏	3. Holds clipboard and stopwatch so child cannot see what he/she records.
❏	❏	4. Starts stopwatch after saying "Begin."
❏	❏	5. Waits 3 seconds for child to produce letter sound or word. After 3 seconds, tells correct sound or word and asks child to try the next sound or word. If child does not respond, asks child to move on to the next sound or word.
❏	❏	6. Underlines letter sounds produced correctly alone or in context, and slashes incorrect letter sounds.
❏	❏	7. Follows Discontinue Rule if child does not get any correct letter sounds in first five words.
❏	❏	8. At the end of 1 minute, places a bracket ( ]) after the last letter sound provided and says, "Stop."
❏	❏	9. Records the number of correctly produced letter sounds.
❏	❏	10. Shadow score with the examiner. Is he/she within 2 points on the final score?

DIBELS Oral Reading Fluency and Retell Fluency[5]

Directions for Administration and Scoring

Target Age Range

	DIBELS Oral Reading Fluency																			

	DIBELS Retell Fluency																			

Beg	Mid	End	Beg	Mid	End	Beg	Mid	End	Beg	Mid	End	Beg	Mid	End	Beg	Mid	End	Beg	Mid	End
Kindergarten			First Grade			Second Grade			Third Grade			Fourth Grade			Fifth Grade			Sixth Grade		

DIBELS Oral Reading Fluency is intended for most children from mid first grade through sixth grade. The benchmark goals are 40 in spring of first grade, 90 in spring of second grade, and 110 in the spring of third grade. Students may need intensive instructional support if they score below 10 in spring of first grade, below 50 in spring of second grade, and below 70 in spring of third grade.

Description

DIBELS Oral Reading Fluency (ORF) is a standardized, individually administered test of accuracy and fluency with connected text. The ORF passages and procedures are based on the program of research and development of Curriculum-Based Measurement (CBM) of reading by Stan Deno and colleagues at the University of Minnesota and using the procedures described in Shinn (1989). A version of CBM Reading also has been published as the *Test of Reading Fluency (TORF)* (Children's Educational Services, 1987b). ORF is a standardized set of passages and administration procedures designed to (1) identify children who may need additional instructional support and (2) monitor progress toward instructional goals. The passages are calibrated for the goal level of reading for each grade level. Student performance is measured by having students read a passage aloud for 1 minute. Words omitted or substituted and hesitations of more than 3 seconds are scored as errors. Words self-corrected within 3 seconds are scored as accurate. The number of correct words per minute from the passage is the oral reading fluency rate.

A series of studies has confirmed the technical adequacy of CBM Reading procedures in general. Test-retest reliabilities for elementary students ranged from .92 to .97; alternate-form reliability of different reading passages drawn from the same level ranged from .89 to .94 (Tindal, Marston, & Deno, 1983). Criterion-related validity studied in eight separate studies in the 1980s reported coefficients ranging from .52 to .91 (Good & Jefferson, 1998).

---

[5] Good, R. H., & Kaminski, R. A., & Dill, S. (2002). DIBELS Oral Reading Fluency. In R. H. Good & R. A. Kaminski (Eds.), *Dynamic Indicators of Basic Early Literacy Skills* (6th ed.). Eugene, OR: Institute for the Development of Educational Achievement. Available: http://dibels.uoregon.edu/.

DIBELS Retell Fluency (RTF) is intended to provide a comprehension check for the ORF assessment. In general, oral reading fluency provides one of the best measures of reading competence, including comprehension, for children in first through sixth grades. The purpose of the RTF measure is to (1) prevent inadvertently learning or practicing a misrule, (2) identify children whose comprehension is not consistent with their fluency, (3) provide an explicit linkage to the core components in the NRP report, and (4) increase the face validity of the ORF.

(1) The misrule that we want to prevent is that speed-reading without attending to meaning is either desirable or the intent of the oral reading fluency measure. With a prompted retell, children will be less likely to conclude that simply reading as fast as they can is the desired behavior, and teachers will be less likely to imply that simply reading as fast as one can is desired.

(2) Teachers frequently are concerned about children who read fluently and do not comprehend. This pattern is infrequent but may apply to some children. This procedure may identify those children without increasing unduly the amount of time spent in the assessment.

(3) The National Reading Panel (2000a) report is clear on the core components of early reading, and DIBELS maps explicitly onto this. Retell Fluency is included to provide a brief measure that corresponds directly to the comprehension core component. The current oral reading fluency measure corresponds about as well as anything to reading comprehension. Retell Fluency provides an additional, explicit score that corresponds to the National Reading Panel core components.

(4) A primary concern teachers have about oral reading fluency is the face validity of the measure. Incorporation of an explicit comprehension check may help teachers feel increasingly comfortable with oral reading fluency.

Guidelines for Interpreting Retell Fluency. Preliminary evidence indicates that the Retell Fluency measures correlate with measures of oral reading fluency at about .59. It appears that children's retell scores may be typically about 50% of their oral reading fluency score and that it is unusual for children reading more than 40 words per minute to have a retell score of 25% or less than their oral reading fluency score. So, a rough general rule may be that, for children whose retell is about 50% of their oral reading fluency score, their oral reading fluency score provides a good overall indication of their reading proficiency, including comprehension. But, for children who are reading over 40 words per minute and whose retell score is 25% or less of their oral reading fluency, their oral reading fluency score alone may not be providing a good indication of their overall reading proficiency. For example, a child reading 60 words correct in one minute would be expected to use about 30 words in his retell of the passage. If his retell is about 30, then an oral reading fluency of 60 is providing a good indication of his reading skills. If his retell is 15 or less, then there may be a comprehension concern that is not represented by his oral fluency.

Materials

Student copy of passage, examiner copy, clipboard, stopwatch, and colored scoring pen.

Directions for Administration—Part 1: Oral Reading Fluency

1. Place the reading passage in front of the student.

2. Place the examiner copy on clipboard and position so that the student cannot see what you record.

3. Say these specific directions to the student:

    Please read this (point) ***out loud. If you get stuck, I will tell you the word so you can keep reading. When I say "Stop," I may ask you to tell me about what you read, so do your best reading. Start here*** (point to the first word of the passage). ***Begin.***

4. Start your stopwatch when the student says the first word of the passage. The title is not counted. If the student fails to say the first word after 3 seconds, tell him/her the word and mark it as incorrect, then start your stopwatch.

5. The maximum time for each word is *3 seconds*. If the student does not provide the word within *3 seconds*, say the word and mark the word as incorrect.

6. Follow along on the examiner copy of the probe. Put a slash (/) over words read incorrectly.

7. At the end of 1 minute, place a bracket ( ]) after the last word provided by the student, stop and reset the stopwatch, and say, ***"Stop."*** Remove the passage.

Directions for Administration—Part 2: Retell Fluency

1. If the student reads 10 or more words correct, administer Part 2: Retell Fluency. Say,

    Please tell me all about what you just read. Try to tell me everything you can. Begin.

2. Start your stopwatch after you say "Begin."

3. Count the number of words the child produces in his or her retell by moving your pen through the dots as the student is responding. Try to record accurately the number of words in the student's response. Put a circle around the total number of words in the student's response.

    Example: If the student says, "The bird had a nest. There was a mommy bird," move your pen through the numbers as the student responds and circle the total words.

10

4. The *first time* the student does not say anything for *3 seconds*, say, **"Try to tell me everything you can."** This prompt can be used *only once*.

5. After the first prompt, if the student does not say anything or gets off track for *5 seconds*, circle the total number of words in the student's retell and say, **"Stop."**

6. At the end of 1 minute, circle the total number of words in the student's retell and say, **"Stop."**

Directions for Scoring—Part 1: Oral Reading Fluency

1. Score reading passages immediately after administration.

2. *Discontinue Rule.* If the student does not read any words correctly in the first row of the first passage, discontinue the task and record a score of zero (0) on the front cover.

3. Record the total number of words read correctly on the bottom of the scoring sheet for each passage.

4. If the student reads fewer than 10 words correct on the first passage, record his/her score on the front cover and do not administer passages 2 and 3.

5. If the student reads 3 passages, record his/her middle score on the front cover. For example, if the student gets scores of 27, 36, and 25, record a score of 27 on the front cover.

6. *Hesitation or Struggle With Words.* If a student hesitates or struggles with a word for 3 seconds, tell the student the word and mark the word as incorrect. If necessary, indicate for the student to continue with the next word.

Passage	Student Says	Scoring Procedure	Correct Words/ Total Words
I have a goldfish.	"I have a … (3 seconds)"	I have a ~~goldfish.~~	**3** /4

7. *Hyphenated Words.* Hyphenated words count as two words if both parts can stand alone as individual words. Hyphenated words count as one word if either part cannot stand alone as an individual word.

Passage	Number of Words
I gave Ben a red yo-yo.	6
We did push-ups, pull-ups, and sit-ups.	9

8. *Numerals.* Numerals must be read correctly in the context of the sentence.

Passage	Student Says	Scoring Procedure	Correct Words/ Total Words
My father is 36.	"My father is thirty-six."	My father is 36.	**4** /4
My father is 36.	"My father is three six."	My father is ~~36.~~	**3** /4
I am 6 years old.	"I am six years old."	I am 6 years old.	**5** /5

9. *Mispronounced Words.* A word is scored as correct if it is pronounced correctly in the context of the sentence. If the word is mispronounced in the context, it is scored as an error.

Passage	Student Says	Scoring Procedure	Correct Words/ Total Words
It was a live fish.	"It was a liv fish" (i.e., with a short "i").	It was a ~~live~~ fish.	**4**/5
I ate too much.	"I eat too much."	I ~~ate~~ too much.	**3**/4

10. *Self-Corrections.* A word is scored as correct if it is initially mispronounced but the student self-corrects within 3 seconds. Mark "SC" above the word and score as correct.

Passage	Student Says	Scoring Procedure	Correct Words/ Total Words
It was a live fish.	"It was a liv … live fish" (i.e., self-corrects to long "i" within 3 sec.).	SC It was a ~~live~~ fish.	**5**/5

11. *Repeated Words.* Words that are repeated are not scored as incorrect and are ignored in scoring.

Passage	Student Says	Scoring Procedure	Correct Words/ Total Words
I have a goldfish.	"I have a … I have a goldfish."	I have a goldfish.	**4**/4

12. *Articulation and Dialect.* The student is not penalized for imperfect pronunciation due to dialect, articulation, or second-language interference. For example, if the student *consistently* says /th/ for /s/, and reads "rest" as "retht," he or she should be given credit for a correct word. This is a professional judgment and should be based on the student's responses and any prior knowledge of his/her speech patterns.

Passage	Student Says	Scoring Procedure	Correct Words/ Total Words
It is time for a rest.	"It is time for a retht." (articulation)	It is time for a rest.	**6**/6
We took the short cut.	"We took the shot cut." (dialect)	We took the short cut.	**5**/5

13. *Inserted Words.* Inserted words are ignored and not counted as errors. The student also does not get additional credit for inserted words. If the student frequently inserts extra words, note the pattern at the bottom of the scoring page.

Passage	Student Says	Scoring Procedure	Correct Words/ Total Words
It is time for a rest.	"It is time for a long rest."	It is time for a rest.	**6**/6
I ate too much.	"I ate way too much."	I ate too much.	**4**/4

14. *Omitted Words.* Omitted words are scored as incorrect.

Passage	Student Says	Scoring Procedure	Correct Words/ Total Words
It is time for a rest.	"It is time for rest."	It is time for a̸ rest.	**5** /6
I ate too much.	"I ate much."	I ate t̸o̸o̸ much.	**3** /4

15. *Word Order.* All words that are read correctly but in the wrong order are scored as incorrect.

Passage	Student Says	Scoring Procedure	Correct Words/ Total Words
The ice cream man comes.	"The cream ice man comes."	The i̸c̸e̸ c̸r̸e̸a̸m̸ man comes.	**3** /5
I ate too much.	"I too ate much."	I a̸t̸e̸ t̸o̸o̸ much.	**2** /4

16. *Abbreviations.* Abbreviations should be read in the way you would normally pronounce the abbreviation in conversation. For example, TV could be read as "teevee" or "television," but Mr. would be read as "mister."

Passage	Student Says	Scoring Procedure	Correct Words/ Total Words
May I watch TV?	"May I watch teevee?"	May I watch TV?	**4** /4
May I watch TV?	"May I watch television?"	May I watch TV?	**4** /4
My teacher is Mr. Smith.	"My teacher is Mister Smith."	My teacher is Mr. Smith.	**5** /5
My teacher is Mr. Smith.	"My teacher is 'm' 'r' Smith."	My teacher is M̸r̸. Smith.	**4** /5

Directions for Scoring—Part 2: Retell Fluency

1. Score retell while the child is responding. Circle total number of words immediately after examiner says, "Stop."

2. *Number of Retell Words.* Count the number of words the child retells that illustrates his/ her understanding of the passage.

3. *Exclamations are not counted.* Only actual words are counted. If the child inserts mazes or other sounds, inserted sounds are not counted.

Passage	Student Says
I love going to the library downtown. There are so many books. There is a big room in the library that is just for kids. I can reach all the books by myself.	They uhh they are going to the uhh library. It is uhhh downtown. uhh There's a room.

⊗ • • • • • • • • * • • ⓧ • • • • • • * • • • • • • • • • • *

13

4. _Count contractions as one word._ For example, if the child uses "She's" or "We'll," they would only count as one word.

Passage	Student Says
I love going to the library downtown. There are so many books. There is a big room in the library that is just for kids. I can reach all the books by myself.	They're going to the library. It's downtown. There's a room.

5. _Songs or recitations are not included._ If the child recites the ABCs or tells a song or poem, even if relevant to the retell, the recitation, song, or poem is not counted.

Passage	Student Says
I love going to the library downtown. There are so many books. There is a big room in the library that is just for kids. I can reach all the books by myself.	They're going to the library. The books have letters like A B C D E F G H I J K L M N O P Q R S T U V W X Y Z.

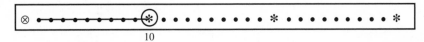

6. _Minor repetitions, redundancies, irrelevancies, and inaccuracies are counted._ The crucial judgment is whether the student is retelling the passage or has gotten off track on another story or topic. In this example, the child (1) goes from "they" to "I", (2) changes "love" to "like," (3) changes the order of events, (4) repeats "library," (5) confuses "room" and "books," and (6) confuses "reach" and "read." However, her retell is fundamentally on track, and all words would count.

Passage	Student Says
I love going to the library downtown. There are so many books. There is a big room in the library that is just for kids. I can reach all the books by myself.	They're going to the library. The library is downtown. I like the library. They have books just for kids. I can read them myself

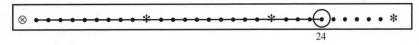

7. _Rote repetitions of words or phrases are not counted._

Passage	Student Says
I love going to the library downtown. There are so many books. There is a big room in the library that is just for kids. I can reach all the books by myself.	(sing-song voice) They're going to the library. They're going to the library. They're going to the library.

8. *Repeating their retell is not counted.* Especially when children are prompted to "try to tell me everything you can," they may simply repeat what they have already provided.

Passage	Student Says
I love going to the library downtown. There are so many books. There is a big room in the library that is just for kids. I can reach all the books by myself.	They're going to the library. Lots of books. [prompt] They're going to the library. Books.

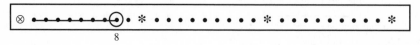

9. *Stories or irrelevancies that are off track are not counted.* Children may start telling something from their own experience that is vaguely related to the passage. Such stories are not counted.

Passage	Student Says
I love going to the library downtown. There are so many books. There is a big room in the library that is just for kids. I can reach all the books by myself.	They're going to the library. They have lots of books. My mom took me to the library. We got Dr. Seuss and *Willy Wonka*. They are my favorite books.

DIBELS Oral Reading Fluency
Assessment Integrity Checklist

Directions: As the observer, please observe setup and directions, time and score the test with the examiner, check examiner's accuracy in following procedures, and decide if examiner passes or needs more practice.

Fine	Needs Practice	√ box to indicate Fine or Needs Practice
❏	❏	1. Performs standardized directions verbatim: *Please read this out loud. If you get stuck, I will tell you the word so you can keep reading. When I say "Stop," I may ask you to tell me about what you read, so do your best reading. Start here. Begin.*
❏	❏	2. Holds clipboard and stopwatch so child cannot see what he/she records.
❏	❏	3. Starts stopwatch after child says the first word of the passage.
❏	❏	4. For first word, waits 3 seconds for child to read the word. After 3 seconds, says the correct word, starts the stopwatch, and scores the first word as incorrect.
❏	❏	5. For all words, if child hesitates or struggles with a word for 3 seconds, says the correct word and scores the word as incorrect.
❏	❏	6. Puts a slash through words read incorrectly.
❏	❏	7. Follows discontinue rule if child does not get any words correct in first 5 words.
❏	❏	8. At the end of 1 minute, places a bracket ( ]) after the last word provided and says, "Stop."
❏	❏	9. Records the number of correct words.
❏	❏	10. Shadow score oral reading fluency with the examiner. Is he/she within 2 points on the final score?
❏	❏	11. Performs retell standardized directions verbatim: *Please tell me all about what you just read. Try to tell me everything you can. Begin.*
❏	❏	12. If the student does not say anything for 3 seconds, says, "Try to tell me everything you can." This prompt can be used only once.
❏	❏	13. If the student does not say anything or gets off track for 5 seconds, circles the total number of words in the student's retell and says, "Stop."
❏	❏	14. At the end of 1 minute, circles the total number of words in the student's retell and says, "Stop."
❏	❏	15. Shadow score the retell with the examiner. Is he/she within 2 points on the final score?

DIBELS Word Use Fluency[6]

Directions for Administration and Scoring

Target Age Range

Word Use Fluency																				
Beg	Mid	End	Beg	Mid	End	Beg	Mid	End	Beg	Mid	End	Beg	Mid	End	Beg	Mid	End	Beg	Mid	End
Kindergarten			First Grade			Second Grade			Third Grade			Fourth Grade			Fifth Grade			Sixth Grade		

Word Use Fluency (WUF) is intended for most children from fall of kindergarten through third grade. A benchmark goal is not provided for WUF because additional research is needed to establish its linkage to other big ideas of early literacy (phonological awareness, alphabetic principle, and accuracy and fluency with connected text). Tentatively, students in the lowest 20 percent of a school district using local norms should be considered at risk for poor language and reading outcomes, and those between the 20th percentile and 40th percentile should be considered at some risk.

Materials

Examiner probe, clipboard, stopwatch, and pencil or pen.

Directions for Administration

1. Place examiner probe on clipboard and position so that student cannot see what you record.

2. Say these specific directions to the student:

   Listen to me use this word: "green." (pause) *"The grass is green." Here is another word: "jump."* (pause) *"I like to jump rope." Your turn to use a word.* (pause) *"Rabbit."*

---

[6] Prior editions were supported, in part, by the Early Childhood Research Institute on Measuring Growth and Development (H180M10006) funded by the U. S. Department of Education, Special Education Programs. The authors acknowledge with appreciation the assistance of Rachel Katz, Jennifer Jeffrey, Katy Kimer, Jennifer Knutson, and Carol Stock.

Good, R. H., Kaminski, R. A., & Smith, S. (2002). Word Use Fluency. In R. H. Good & R. A. Kaminski (Eds.), *Dynamic Indicators of Basic Early Literacy Skills* (6th ed.). Eugene, OR: Institute for the Development of Educational Achievement. Available: http://dibels.uoregon.edu/.

CORRECT RESPONSE: If student uses the word correctly in a phrase, say	INCORRECT RESPONSE: If student gives any other response, say
Very good.	*Listen to me use the word "rabbit."* (pause) *"The rabbit is eating a carrot." Your turn. "Rabbit."*

OK. Here is your first word.

3. Give the student the first word and start your stopwatch. If the student does not begin to use the word after *5 seconds*, give him/her the second word and score the first word as zero.

4. Provide the next word when the student has used the word in a phrase, expression, or utterance or when the student hesitates or pauses for *5 seconds*. As soon as the student is finished using the word, present the next word promptly and clearly.

5. At the end of 1 minute, stop presenting words and recording further responses. Count the number of words used correctly in phrases, expressions, or sentences, and record at the end of the row. Total these scores and record at the bottom of the scoring sheet.

Directions for Scoring

1. The total score will be the total number of words used correctly in an utterance. An utterance may be a phrase, expression, definition, or sentence. For each target word, the words in the final and/or most complete utterance will be counted.

2. *Number of Words.* Count the number of words the child produces in response to a word by moving your pen through the numbers as the student is responding. Try to record accurately the number of words in the student's response. Put a circle around the total number of words in the student's response.

   - Count only actual words, not exclamations like "um."
   - Score contractions (e.g., "She's," "We'll") as one word.
   - Words do not include songs or recitations (e.g., the ABCs and 1, 2, 3, etc.) performed either individually or in a group.
   - If a child perseverates on a word (e.g., "beep, beep, beep, beep"), count the word as a single-word utterance (if it is the only word stated by a child) or as one word in a multiword utterance.

   Example: If the word is "stone," and the student says "I threw the stone in the water," move your pen through the numbers as the student responds and circle the total words.

stone	0 1 2 3 4 5 6 ⑦ 8 9 10 11 12 13 14 15 16 17 18 19 20	_____ C I

3. *Correct Utterance.* Mark the usage of the word in an utterance as correct or incorrect. Correct utterances are scored liberally. If the utterance conveys the accurate meaning of the word and could be correct, score it as correct. A response is considered correct when it meets the requirement for either correct use or correct definition.

    - Correct Use: For an utterance to be considered correct in terms of use, the target word is used correctly in a phrase, expression, or sentence.

    - Correct Definition: Correct definitions are accepted as a correct utterance. Correct definitions do not need to contain the target word to be accepted as correct. Synonyms are considered definitions.

4. *Total Number of Words in Correct Utterances.* At the end of 1 minute, add up the number of words in each correct utterance to obtain the total number of words in correct utterances. *Note: Do not count words used in incorrect responses. Count the number of words used in correct utterances only.*

5. *Discontinue Rule.* If a student has not used any of the first 5 words correctly in a phrase, expression, or sentence, discontinue the task and put a score of zero (0).

Scoring Examples

Correct Use

1. *Correct Use.* If the word is used in a phrase, expression, or sentence and conveys the meaning of the word, the response is correct.

    Example: If the word is "stone," and the student says, "I threw the stone in the water," circle the total words, mark the utterance as correct, and write the total number of words in the blank.

| stone | 0 1 2 3 4 5 6 ⑦ 8 9 10 11 12 13 14 15 16 17 18 19 20 | 7 Ⓒ I |

    Example: If the word is "school," and the student says, "I like school because it's fun," circle the total words, mark the utterance as correct, and write the total number of words in the blank.

| school | 0 1 2 3 4 5 ⑥ 7 8 9 10 11 12 13 14 15 16 17 18 19 20 | 6 Ⓒ I |

2. *False starts within a correct use are not counted.*

Example: If the word is "school," and the student says, "School. I like school. I like school because it's fun," score the final/most complete utterance only. Circle the number of words in the final utterance, mark the utterance as correct, and write the total number of words in the blank.

school	0̶ 1̶ 2̶ 3̶ 4̶ 5̶ ⑥7 8 9 10 11 12 13 14 15 16 17 18 19 20	_6_ Ⓒ I

3. *Repetitions of words or phrases within a correct use are not counted.*

Example: If the student says, "School… school… I like … I like … I like school because it's fun," circle the total words in the final/most complete utterance ("I like school because it's fun"), mark the utterance as correct, and write the total number of words in the blank.

school	0̶ 1̶ 2̶ 3̶ 4̶ 5̶⑥7 8 9 10 11 12 13 14 15 16 17 18 19 20	_6_ Ⓒ I

4. *Words used as fillers within a correct use are not counted.*

Example: If the student says, "School…um…well…you know…um…I…um…like school because it's…um…you know…fun," circle the total words in the final/most complete utterance ("I like school because it's fun"), mark the utterance as correct, and write the total number of words in the blank.

school	0̶ 1̶ 2̶ 3̶ 4̶ 5̶⑥7 8 9 10 11 12 13 14 15 16 17 18 19 20	_6_ Ⓒ I

5. *Homophones.* Correct use of a homophone is scored as correct. Use of a word that sounds the same as the target word would be counted as a correct use.

Example: If the word is "board," and the student says, "I am bored," circle the total words, mark the utterance as correct, and write the total number of words in the blank.

board	0̶ 1̶ 2̶③4 5 6 7 8 9 10 11 12 13 14 15 16 17 18 19 20	_3_ Ⓒ I

DIBELS Word Use Fluency
© 2003 All Rights Reserved

6. *Correct definition is scored as a correct use.* A correct definition or synonym conveys the meaning of the word and would be counted as a correct use.

Example: If the word is "stone," and the student says, "Something that is round and hard," circle the total words, mark the utterance as correct, and write the total number of words in the blank.

stone	0 1 2 3 4 5 ⑥ 7 8 9 10 11 12 13 14 15 16 17 18 19 20	_6_ Ⓒ I

Example: If the word is "red," and the student says, "color," a definition or synonym would be scored as a correct use, even if it is only one word. Circle the total words, mark the utterance as correct, and write the total number of words.

red	0 ① 2 3 4 5 6 7 8 9 10 11 12 13 14 15 16 17 18 19 20	_1_ Ⓒ I

Non-example: If the word is "red," and the student says, "robin," the word "robin" is not a correct use or definition of the target word, "red." Circle the total words and mark the utterance as incorrect.

red	⓪ 1 2 3 4 5 6 7 8 9 10 11 12 13 14 15 16 17 18 19 20	_0_ C Ⓘ

Example: Target word is "red," and the student says, "red robin," circle the total words, mark the utterance as correct, and write the total number of words.

red	0 1 ② 3 4 5 6 7 8 9 10 11 12 13 14 15 16 17 18 19 20	_2_ Ⓒ I

7. *Changing Tense, Number, or Parts of Speech.* If the student changes the tense or number of the word and uses the word correctly in an utterance, score as correct.

Example: If the word is "stone," and the student says, "Don't throw stones," circle the total words, mark the utterance as correct, and write the total number of words in the blank.

stone	0 1 2 ③ 4 5 6 7 8 9 10 11 12 13 14 15 16 17 18 19 20	_3_ Ⓒ I

Example: The word is "dress," and the student says, "get dressed." "Dress" can be used correctly as a verb (to put clothing on) and as a noun (dress as a piece of clothing). Circle the total words, mark the utterance as correct, and write the total number of words in the blank.

dress	0 1 ② 3 4 5 6 7 8 9 10 11 12 13 14 15 16 17 18 19 20	_2_ Ⓒ I

8. *Long Response or Multiple Utterances.* Count only the words in the most complete utterance in which the target word was used. Stop counting and redirect the student back to the task by providing the next word.

Example: The word is "stone," and the student says, "I like to throw stones in the morning, and I especially like to throw stones when we go fishing. I went fishing with my dad this weekend, and we didn't catch anything at all. I was sad and my dad was too." Circle the total words in the first utterance in which the target word was used, mark the utterance as correct, and write the total number of words in the blank.

| stone | 0 1 2 3 4 5 6 7 8 9 10 11 12 13 14 15 16 17 18 ⑲ 20 | 19 Ⓒ I |

Incorrect Usage

1. *Incorrect Response.* The target word is used in the response, but the response does not make sense. The word is used incorrectly or the utterance does not convey the accurate meaning of the word.

Example: If the word is "stone," and the student says, "I like to eat stones for lunch," circle the total words and mark the utterance as incorrect.

| stone | 0 1 2 3 4 5 6 ⑦ 8 9 10 11 12 13 14 15 16 17 18 19 20 | 0 C Ⓘ |

Example: If the word is "school," and the student says, "I school my jumps," circle the total words and mark the utterance as incorrect.

| school | 0 1 2 3 ④ 5 6 7 8 9 10 11 12 13 14 15 16 17 18 19 20 | 0 C Ⓘ |

2. *Repeating the target word is not a correct use.* Simply repeating the word does not convey or imply correct meaning or use of the word, and would be scored as an incorrect use.

Example: If the word is "school," and the student says, "School," circle the total words and mark the phrase or utterance as incorrect.

| school | 0 ① 2 3 4 5 6 7 8 9 10 11 12 13 14 15 16 17 18 19 20 | 0 C Ⓘ |

3. *No Response.* If student doesn't respond in 5 seconds, circle zero, proceed to the next word and score as incorrect.

Example: If the word is "stone," and the student does not say any words, circle the zero and mark the phrase or utterance as incorrect.

| stone | ⓪ 1 2 3 4 5 6 7 8 9 10 11 12 13 14 15 16 17 18 19 20 | 0 C Ⓘ |

4. *"I don't know."* If the student says, "I don't know that one," circle zero, proceed to the next word, and score as incorrect.

Example: If the word is "stone," and the student says, "I don't know that one," circle the total words and mark the phrase or utterance as incorrect.

stone	⓪ 1 2 3 4 5 6 7 8 9 10 11 12 13 14 15 16 17 18 19 20	0 C Ⓘ

DIBELS Approved Accommodations

The purpose of accommodations is to facilitate assessment for children for whom a standard administration may not provide an accurate estimate of their skills in the core early literacy skill areas. Assessment and accommodations to assessment should be consistent with the primary goal of accurately estimating the child's skills in phonemic awareness, phonics or alphabetic principle, accuracy and fluency with connected text, reading comprehension, and vocabulary development.

DIBELS-approved accommodations are accommodations that are unlikely to change substantially the meaning or interpretation of scores on the measures or the target skill being assessed by the measure. When DIBELS-approved accommodations are used, the regular DIBELS interpretation guidelines apply, and the scores can be entered into the DIBELS Data System for reporting and interpretation. The "Tested with DIBELS-Approved Accommodations" box should be checked in the student demographics section.

When the DIBELS assessments are administered in ways different from both a DIBELS standard administration and the DIBELS-approved accommodations, the administration would be considered an unstandardized administration and the resulting scores cannot be interpreted with the DIBELS interpretive and reporting procedures. Scores from a nonstandard administration using unapproved accommodations should not be entered into the DIBELS Data System for reporting and analysis. For example, extended time or untimed administration would *not* be a DIBELS-approved accommodation. For the DIBELS measures, fluency is an integral aspect of the construct being assessed. Scores from an untimed administration would not be comparable or interpretable with the procedures for reporting and interpreting DIBELS scores. An interventionist may elect to administer the DIBELS in an untimed way, but the scores should not be entered into the DIBELS Data System, the reliability and validity data for DIBELS would not be applicable, and the benchmark goals would not be relevant or appropriate.

Changes in Test Administration and Scoring That are Not Approved Accommodations

Timing. Changes in the timing of DIBELS assessments or untimed administrations are not approved accommodations. If the DIBELS measures are administered under untimed conditions or with extended time, the scores should not be entered into the DIBELS Data System. In addition, the research establishing the reliability and validity of the measures would not apply to untimed or extended time administrations, and the scoring guidelines for interpreting level of risk and for making instructional recommendations would not apply.

Approved Accommodations for Retesting and Test-Teach-Test	ISF	PSF	NWF	ORF	LNF	WUF
A powerful accommodation for students who experience a variety of difficulties is to repeat the assessment under different conditions or with different testers. Retesting should take place on *different days* with *different probes* under *different conditions* that are considered to potentially impact student performance. The median of the three most recent assessments should be used as the best indicator of the child's skills.	X	X	X	X	X	X
Response to instruction is a second, powerful accommodation for students who experience a variety of difficulties. Repeat assessment on *different days* with *different probes* in the context of explicit instruction on the target skills. The target skills are phonemic awareness, phonics, and accuracy and fluency with text. *The target skills should be explicitly taught. Under no conditions should the specific items on a probe be explicitly taught.* The median of the three most recent assessments should be used as the best indicator of the child's skills.	X	X	X	X	X	X

Approved Accommodations for Setting and Tester	ISF	PSF	NWF	ORF	LNF	WUF
The child may be tested in an alternate setting. For example, a special room with minimal distractions, complete quiet, or enhanced or specialized lighting may be used.	X	X	X	X	X	X
The child may be tested with a familiar person, interpreter, specialist, or other facilitator present. The familiar person or interpreter may assist in supporting the student and tester to obtain an accurate estimate of the student's skills.	X	X	X	X	X	X
The child may be tested by a tester with whom the child is comfortable and who is familiar with the child's language and communicative strategies, for example, the child's teacher, or an aide especially familiar to the child, or even the child's parent. In all cases the tester must receive appropriate training, observation, and supervision.	X	X	X	X	X	X
The child may be tested by a professional with relevant specialized training. For example, a child with severe articulation difficulty might be tested by a speech-language pathologist. Appropriate training is essential.	X	X	X	X	X	X

Approved Accommodations for Directions	ISF	PSF	NWF	ORF	LNF	WUF
The practice item may be repeated or one additional example may be provided.	X	X	X			X
If necessary, the child can be provided with a lead example in addition to the model example. "The sounds in 'sam' are /s/ /a/ /m/. Do it with me, /s/ /a/ /m/."	X	X	X			
The child's understanding of directions can be checked. For example, the child can be asked to repeat or summarize the directions.	X	X	X	X	X	X
The directions can be provided in a manner more accessible to the child. For example, directions can be provided in sign language for a child who would be more comfortable with signed directions than verbal directions. A child with limited English proficiency may be provided with the directions in their primary language. For example, to assess a child's early literacy skills in English, directions for the task may be provided in Spanish and stimulus items presented in English.	X	X	X	X	X	X

Approved Accommodations for Stimulus Materials	ISF	PSF	NWF	ORF	LNF	WUF
Large print or an enlarged edition of stimulus materials may be used.	X		X	X	X	
Closed-circuit TV for enlargement of print and picture stimuli is appropriate if necessary to enhance performance for students with low vision.	X		X	X	X	
Colored overlays, filters, or lighting is appropriate if vision and performance are enhanced.	X		X	X	X	
If a student has sufficient skills with Braille, a Braille edition of stimulus materials may be used. A Braille edition of materials is in development. Scores for the Braille edition may not be directly comparable.			X	X	X	
An alternate font for stimulus materials may be used. For example, most print materials use a Times font for reading materials in first and second grade. The target for any font is one that would be used in reading materials in first grade.			X	X	X	
Stimulus materials may be printed in color for ease of identification and use.	X					
Alternate pictures of the target words may be used if pictures that are more familiar to the student are available. The target word should not be changed.	X					

	ISF	PSF	NWF	ORF	LNF	WUF
If the words used in the Initial Sound Fluency are unfamiliar vocabulary for the student, the student can be asked to repeat the word associated with each picture. For example, "This is mouse. What is this? This is flowers. What is this? This is pillow. What is this? This is letters. What is this?"	X					
If the words used in the Initial Sound Fluency are unfamiliar vocabulary for the student, the vocabulary can be pretaught prior to administration of the measure. The words selected for the ISF measure are drawn from written materials appropriate for first and second grade students, so students can be expected to encounter the words in their reading.	X					
Amplification or a direct sound system from tester to student is appropriate if it will facilitate hearing of directions or test stimuli.	X	X	X	X	X	X
Approved Accommodations for Student Responses	ISF	PSF	NWF	ORF	LNF	WUF
If necessary to facilitate student responding, the student or tester may have a marker or ruler under a line of text or items in order to focus attention. This accommodation should only be used if necessary for the student to respond. In a standard administration, if the student skips a row, the row is not counted or penalized, and instructionally relevant information on the student's tracking skills is obtained.			X	X	X	
The student may respond using a preferred or strongest mode of communication. For example, the student may sign, use a word board, or use a computer to use a word or read a passage. The tester should make a professional judgment regarding the fluency of response. If the student's fluency is affected by the accommodation, then the standard scoring rules should not be applied.				X		X

DIBELS Instructional Recommendations:
Intensive, Strategic, and Benchmark[7]

The purpose of this technical report is to provide a compilation of the Dynamic Indicators of Basic Early Literacy Skills (DIBELS) (Good & Kaminski, 2002) decision rules for intensive, strategic, and benchmark instructional recommendations. These decision rules represent a revision of the initial decision rules used in the DIBELS Data System. The initial decision rules focused on the longitudinal predictive validity of specific benchmark goals: Initial Sound Fluency (ISF) in middle of kindergarten, Phoneme Segmentation Fluency (PSF) at the end of kindergarten, Nonsense Word Fluency (NWF) in middle of first grade, and DIBELS Oral Reading Fluency (ORF) at the end of first, second, and third grades. The revised decision rules utilize the longitudinal predictive information from all participants in the DIBELS Data System to identify progressive benchmark goals en route to the initial goals. Within-academic-year predictive utilities are based on all schools participating in the DIBELS Data System during the 2001–2002 academic year. For example, the predictive utility of a beginning kindergarten recommendation for an end of kindergarten goal would be a within-year utility. Across-year predictive utilities are based on all schools participating in the DIBELS Data System during the 2000–2001 and 2001–2002 academic years. For example, the predictive utility of a beginning kindergarten recommendation for an end of first grade goal would be an across-year predictive utility.

In establishing the DIBELS decision rules and instructional recommendations, we followed some general rules and principles. A first guiding principle is that we wanted to establish cutoffs and goals for healthy reading outcomes where the odds would be in favor of achieving subsequent early literacy goals and outcomes. For individual indicators, the level of performance where the odds are in favor of achieving subsequent outcomes was referred to as *low risk* if the measure was administered prior to the benchmark goal, and it was referred to as *established* if the measure was administered at the time of the benchmark goal or after. When all available information from the DIBELS Benchmark Assessment is considered and an overall recommendation made, patterns of performance with the odds in favor of achieving subsequent goals received a recommendation of *Benchmark - At grade level*. In general, we tried to establish cutoffs and rules where the odds in favor of achieving subsequent goals meant that approximately 80 percent or more of students with the pattern would achieve the goal.

A secondary goal of the decision rules was to identify students with the odds against achieving subsequent early literacy goals for whom intervention would be indicated. We tried to establish cutoffs where the odds against meant that approximately 20 percent or fewer of students with

---

[7] This report supported in part by the Center for Improving Reading Competence Using Intensive Treatments Schoolwide (Project CIRCUITS) funded by the U. S. Department of Education, Office of Special Education Programs (CFDA 84.324X).

Good, R. H., Simmons, D. Kame'enui, E. Kaminski, R. A., & Wallin, J. (2002). DIBELS instructional recommendations: Intensive, strategic, and benchmark. In R. H. Good & R. A. Kaminski (Eds.), *Dynamic Indicators of Basic Early Literacy Skills* (6th ed.). Eugene, OR: Institute for the Development of Educational Achievement. Available: http://dibels.uoregon.edu/.

the pattern would achieve subsequent goals. For individual indicators, the level of performance where the odds are against achieving subsequent goals was referred to as *at risk* if the measure was administered prior to the benchmark goal and *deficit* if the measure was administered at the benchmark goal or later. An instructional recommendation based on all of the DIBELS Benchmark Assessment measures for students with the odds against achieving subsequent goals was *Intensive - Needs Substantial Intervention*.

The third level of performance was when a clear prediction was not possible. In this case, the odds would be neither in favor nor against. We tried to establish cutoffs for the middle category where approximately 50 percent of students achieved subsequent early literacy goals. For individual indicators, the middle category was referred to as *some risk* prior to a benchmark goal, and *emerging* at a benchmark goal or later. When the pattern of performance across all of the DIBELS Benchmark Assessment measures did not yield a clear prediction, i.e., 50-50 odds, the instructional recommendation was *Strategic - Additional Intervention*.

On an individual measure basis, multiple factors were considered when establishing the cutoff points. The primary consideration was the odds of achieving subsequent early literacy goals. An additional factor that was considered was the percent of students in each decision category. A rough target was 20 percent to be identified as at risk or intensive, and 20 percent identified as some risk or strategic. A rough goal of effective reform would be 5 percent requiring intensive instructional intervention and 15 percent requiring strategic instructional support so that 100 percent achieve benchmark early literacy goals.

For each individual measure, Receiver Operator Characteristic (ROC) curves were examined to identify the tradeoff in sensitivity and specificity for possible cut scores. For each measure, ROC curves were generated and evaluated for relevant subsequent benchmark goals. For example, in the beginning of kindergarten, ROC curves were examined for four benchmark goals: (a) ISF in middle of kindergarten, (b) PSF in end of kindergarten, (c) NWF in middle of first grade, and (d) ORF in end of first grade. For each measure and each benchmark goal, two ROC curves were considered: (a) with respect to a goal outcome of reading health (i.e., odds in favor of achieving subsequent goals), and (b) with respect to a goal outcome of reading difficulty (i.e., the level of the goal with odds against achieving subsequent goals). So, for example, for ISF at the beginning of kindergarten, eight different ROC curves were considered and evaluated.

An additional consideration in establishing DIBELS decision rules and instructional recommendations was the theoretical structure and linkage of beginning reading skills with respect to literacy outcomes. Needless to say, it was seldom possible to establish a decision rule that satisfied all of these factors and considerations equally. A tradeoff of desirable features was frequently required. The overarching priority was to establish instructional recommendations and instructional goals where the odds are in favor of achieving subsequent literacy outcomes. Complete information on the development and specification of these decision rules is in preparation as CIRCUITS Technical Reports 1 through 11 and should be available by January, 2004.

Beginning of Kindergarten Instructional Recommendation

The specific cutoffs for the DIBELS Benchmark Assessment measures in the beginning of kindergarten are reported in Table 1. For example, students with ISF less than 4 would be at risk, and students with ISF of 8 or more would be at low risk. The DIBELS instructional recommendations and the percent of students with each DIBELS pattern who achieve subsequent goals is reported in Table 2. For each DIBELS pattern, at risk on ISF and at risk on LNF for example, the percent of students with the pattern who achieve each subsequent early literacy goal is provided. For example, of the students who are at risk on both ISF and LNF, 9 percent achieved the ISF goal in middle of kindergarten, 44 percent achieved the PSF goal at the end of kindergarten, 24 percent achieved the NWF goal in the middle of first grade, and 34 percent achieved the ORF goal at the end of first grade. The average column is the average percent achieving subsequent goals. The patterns of performance are ordered by the average percent achieving subsequent goals. For each pattern, the percentile rank for the pattern is provided. For example, a student who is at risk on both ISF and LNF is at the 3rd percentile compared to other students in the DIBELS Data System. This means they scored as well as or better than 3 percent of students in the DIBELS Data System in the beginning of kindergarten. Percentile ranks were computed by adding one half of the percent of students with the same pattern plus the percent of students in patterns with a lower average achieving subsequent goals (Salvia & Ysseldyke, 2001).

Table 1

Descriptive Levels of Performance in Beginning of Kindergarten

Measure	Performance	Descriptor
DIBELS Initial Sound Fluency	ISF < 4	At Risk
	4 <= ISF < 8	Some Risk
	ISF >= 8	Low Risk
DIBELS Letter Naming Fluency	LNF < 2	At Risk
	2 <= LNF < 8	Some Risk
	LNF >= 8	Low Risk

Table 2

Instructional Recommendations for Individual Patterns of Performance on Beginning of Kindergarten DIBELS Benchmark Assessment

| Initial Sound Fluency | Letter Naming Fluency | Percent Meeting Later Goals | | | | | | Incidence | Instructional Support Recommendation |
		Pctile	Mid K ISF	End K PSF	Mid I NWF	End I ORF	Avg.		
At Risk	At Risk	3	9	44	24	34	27	More Common	Intensive - Needs Substantial Intervention
Some Risk	At Risk	9	13	48	27	31	30	More Common	Intensive - Needs Substantial Intervention
At Risk	Some Risk	13	13	53	32	44	35	More Common	Intensive - Needs Substantial Intervention
Some Risk	Some Risk	19	18	58	33	45	39	More Common	Strategic - Additional Intervention
Low Risk	At Risk	25	26	57	30	43	39	More Common	Strategic - Additional Intervention
Low Risk	Some Risk	33	35	68	43	56	51	More Common	Strategic - Additional Intervention
At Risk	Low Risk	42	23	59	50	74	51	More Common	Strategic - Additional Intervention
Some Risk	Low Risk	50	30	71	51	75	57	More Common	Strategic - Additional Intervention
Low Risk	Low Risk	76	62	83	69	87	75	More Common	Benchmark - At grade level

© 2002 Dynamic Measurement Group, Inc.

Note: Percent meeting goal is the conditional percent of children who meet the (a) middle kindergarten goal of 25 on ISF, (b) end of kindergarten goal of 35 on PSF, (c) middle of first grade goal of 50 on NWF, and (d) end of first grade goal of 40 or more on DIBELS ORF.

The incidence column in Table 2 is intended to provide an indication of how often the pattern of performance occurs. In later decision rules, some patterns of performance are extremely rare. In the beginning of kindergarten, all patterns of performance were more common.

Middle of Kindergarten Instructional Recommendation

The cut scores for the middle of kindergarten Benchmark Assessment are reported in Table 3, and the corresponding instructional recommendations for all patterns of performance are reported in Table 4. The NWF measure is optional in the middle of kindergarten, and so it is not incorporated in the patterns of performance and corresponding instructional recommendations. In the middle of kindergarten, the benchmark goal is 25 or better on ISF, so descriptors for ISF are established, emerging, and benchmark. For the other measures, there is no instructional benchmark goal (LNF) or the measures are administered before the benchmark goal (PSF, NWF), so the descriptors are "at risk," "some risk," and "low risk."

The instructional recommendations in Table 4 are based on the pattern of performance on ISF, LNF, and PSF. The goal is established skills on ISF in the middle of kindergarten, and some patterns with established ISF skills have very good odds of achieving later reading goals. For example, for children who have established initial sounds on ISF and who are low risk on LNF and PSF, the odds are 93 percent of achieving the first grade ORF goal. For other patterns with established initial sounds on ISF, the odds are much lower, resulting in recommendations of strategic instructional support. For example, students with established skills on ISF but who are at risk on LNF and PSF have odds of only 31 percent of achieving the first grade ORF benchmark goal. However, ISF established, LNF at risk, and PSF at risk is an extremely rare and implausible pattern. When a student is very proficient with initial sounds, they should be scoring much higher than 7 on the phoneme segmentation fluency measure, in particular.

Table 3
Descriptive Levels of Performance in Middle of Kindergarten

Measure	Performance	Descriptor
DIBELS Initial Sound Fluency	ISF < 10	Deficit
	10 <= ISF < 25	Emerging
	ISF >= 25	Established
DIBELS Letter Naming Fluency	LNF < 15	At Risk
	15 <= LNF < 27	Some Risk
	LNF >= 27	Low Risk
DIBELS Phoneme Segmentation Fluency	PSF < 7	At Risk
	7 <= PSF < 18	Some Risk
	PSF >= 18	Low Risk
DIBELS Nonsense Word Fluency	NWF < 5	At Risk
	5 <= NWF < 13	Some Risk
	NWF >= 13	Low Risk

Table 4

Instructional Recommendations for Individual Patterns of Performance on Middle of Kindergarten DIBELS Benchmark Assessment

Initial Sound Fluency	Letter Naming Fluency	Phoneme Segmentation Fluency	Pctile	Percent Meeting Later Goals				Incidence	Instructional Support Recommendation
				End K PSF	Mid I NWF	End I ORF	Avg. ORF		
Deficit	At Risk	At Risk	3	18	14	19	17	More Common	Intensive - Needs Substantial Intervention
Deficit	At Risk	Some Risk	7	34	13	21	23	Unusual	Intensive - Needs Substantial Intervention
Emerging	At Risk	At Risk	9	28	20	28	25	More Common	Intensive - Needs Substantial Intervention
Emerging	At Risk	Some Risk	11	41	17	22	27	More Common	Intensive - Needs Substantial Intervention
Deficit	Some Risk	At Risk	13	24	28	48	33	More Common	Intensive - Needs Substantial Intervention
Deficit	At Risk	Low Risk	15	60	21	25	35	Unusual	Intensive - Needs Substantial Intervention
Deficit	Some Risk	Some Risk	16	37	30	40	36	Unusual	Strategic - Additional Intervention
Established	At Risk	At Risk	17	45	32	31	36	Extremely Rare	Strategic - Additional Intervention
Emerging	Some Risk	At Risk	18	37	30	49	38	Unusual	Strategic - Additional Intervention
Deficit	Low Risk	At Risk	20	30	37	58	42	Unusual	Strategic - Additional Intervention
Established	Some Risk	At Risk	21	42	38	49	43	Extremely Rare	Strategic - Additional Intervention
Emerging	Some Risk	Some Risk	22	47	36	51	45	More Common	Strategic - Additional Intervention
Established	Some Risk	Some Risk	24	52	38	47	45	Extremely Rare	Strategic - Additional Intervention
Emerging	At Risk	Low Risk	26	75	29	36	47	More Common	Strategic - Additional Intervention
Deficit	Low Risk	Some Risk	28	43	42	68	51	Unusual	Strategic - Additional Intervention
Deficit	Some Risk	Low Risk	29	66	41	55	54	Extremely Rare	Strategic - Additional Intervention
Emerging	Low Risk	At Risk	31	42	50	70	54	More Common	Strategic - Additional Intervention
Established	Some Risk	Some Risk	33	55	44	64	54	Unusual	Strategic - Additional Intervention
Established	At Risk	Low Risk	34	82	34	47	54	Unusual	Strategic - Additional Intervention
Emerging	Low Risk	Some Risk	38	53	53	80	62	More Common	Strategic - Additional Intervention
Emerging	Some Risk	Low Risk	44	82	47	59	63	More Common	Strategic - Additional Intervention
Established	Low Risk	At Risk	47	51	58	89	66	Extremely Rare	Benchmark - At grade level
Established	Low Risk	Some Risk	49	58	62	87	69	More Common	Benchmark - At grade level
Deficit	Low Risk	Low Risk	52	74	60	75	70	Unusual	Benchmark - At grade level
Established	Some Risk	Low Risk	54	88	56	69	71	More Common	Benchmark - At grade level
Emerging	Low Risk	Low Risk	64	88	68	83	80	More Common	Benchmark - At grade level
Established	Low Risk	Low Risk	86	93	80	93	89	More Common	Benchmark - At grade level

Note: Percent meeting goal is the conditional percent of children who meet the end of first grade goal of 40 or more on DIBELS ORF. Based on *n* of approximately 32,000 students, 638 schools, and 255 school districts.

End of Kindergarten Instructional Recommendation

The end of kindergarten cut scores for risk and established skills are summarized in Table 5, and the instructional recommendations for patterns of DIBELS performance at the end of kindergarten are summarized in Table 6. At the end of kindergarten, it appears to be important for students to have established phonemic awareness on PSF and to be at low risk on NWF with a score of 25 or higher to be confident that the student has the odds in favor of achieving subsequent literacy goals. For most students who achieved 35 on PSF and 25 on NWF, the odds of achieving first grade reading outcomes were 68 percent to 92 percent. Only those students who had the pattern PSF established, NWF low risk, and LNF at risk (an unusual pattern) had odds of about 50-50 of achieving subsequent literacy goals.

Table 5

Descriptive Levels of Performance in End of Kindergarten

Measure	Performance	Descriptor
DIBELS Letter Naming Fluency	LNF < 29	At Risk
	29 <= LNF < 40	Some Risk
	LNF >= 40	Low Risk
DIBELS Phoneme Segmentation Fluency	PSF < 10	Deficit
	10 <= PSF < 35	Emerging
	PSF >= 35	Established
DIBELS Nonsense Word Fluency	NWF < 15	At Risk
	15 <= NWF < 25	Some Risk
	NWF >= 25	Low Risk

Table 6

Instructional Recommendations for Individual Patterns of Performance on End of Kindergarten DIBELS Benchmark Assessment

Letter Naming Fluency	Phoneme Segmentation Fluency	Nonsense Word Fluency	Pctile	Percent Meeting Later Goals			Incidence	Instructional Support Recommendation
				Middle 1 NWF	End 1 ORF	Average		
At Risk	Deficit	At Risk	2	8	19	13	More Common	Intensive - Needs Substantial Intervention
At Risk	Emerging	At Risk	6	15	24	19	More Common	Intensive - Needs Substantial Intervention
At Risk	Established	At Risk	10	17	25	21	More Common	Intensive - Needs Substantial Intervention
At Risk	Deficit	Some Risk	12	21	27	24	Extremely Rare	Intensive - Needs Substantial Intervention
At Risk	Established	Some Risk	13	27	33	30	More Common	Intensive - Needs Substantial Intervention
At Risk	Emerging	Some Risk	15	27	37	32	Unusual	Intensive - Needs Substantial Intervention
Some Risk	Deficit	At Risk	16	22	43	33	Unusual	Intensive - Needs Substantial Intervention
At Risk	Emerging	Low Risk	17	28	39	33	Extremely Rare	Strategic - Additional Intervention
Some Risk	Established	At Risk	18	26	46	36	Unusual	Strategic - Additional Intervention
Some Risk	Emerging	At Risk	20	28	46	37	More Common	Strategic - Additional Intervention
Some Risk	Deficit	Some Risk	22	24	56	40	Extremely Rare	Strategic - Additional Intervention
Some Risk	Emerging	Some Risk	23	35	55	45	More Common	Strategic - Additional Intervention
At Risk	Established	Low Risk	25	40	52	46	Unusual	Strategic - Additional Intervention
Low Risk	Deficit	At Risk	26	34	64	49	Extremely Rare	Strategic - Additional Intervention
At Risk	Deficit	Low Risk	27	36	63	49	Extremely Rare	Strategic - Additional Intervention
Low Risk	Emerging	At Risk	28	34	65	50	Unusual	Strategic - Additional Intervention
Some Risk	Established	Some Risk	30	41	60	50	More Common	Strategic - Additional Intervention
Some Risk	Deficit	Low Risk	33	41	62	51	Extremely Rare	Strategic - Additional Intervention
Low Risk	Deficit	Some Risk	33	41	65	53	Extremely Rare	Strategic - Additional Intervention
Some Risk	Emerging	Low Risk	35	53	65	59	More Common	Strategic - Additional Intervention
Some Risk	Established	Low Risk	38	56	68	62	More Common	Benchmark - At grade level
Low Risk	Established	At Risk	42	46	81	63	Unusual	Benchmark - At grade level
Low Risk	Emerging	Some Risk	44	51	79	65	More Common	Benchmark - At grade level
Low Risk	Established	Some Risk	48	52	79	66	More Common	Benchmark - At grade level
Low Risk	Deficit	Low Risk	52	59	80	69	Extremely Rare	Benchmark - At grade level
Low Risk	Emerging	Low Risk	55	68	87	78	More Common	Benchmark - At grade level
Low Risk	Established	Low Risk	79	81	92	87	More Common	Benchmark - At grade level

Note: Percent meeting goal is the conditional percent of children who meet the end of first grade goal of 40 or more on DIBELS ORF. Based on *n* of approximately 32,000 students, 638 schools, and 255 school districts.

Beginning of First Grade Instructional Recommendation

The cut scores for risk and established skills for the beginning of first grade are summarized in Table 7. A summer effect is apparent in that NWF of 25 is required for low risk at the end of kindergarten, but NWF of 24 is sufficient for low risk at the beginning of first grade. A similar pattern is noticeable for LNF. The instructional recommendation for each pattern of performance at the beginning of first grade is provided in Table 8. As with the end of kindergarten patterns, established skills on PSF and low risk on NWF appear to be important instructional targets for students to be on track for reading outcomes. Even for students who are at risk on LNF, if they achieve the 35 on PSF and 24 on NWF, the odds are 56 percent of achieving the first grade reading goal (an unusual pattern with a strategic support instructional recommendation).

Table 7

Descriptive Levels of Performance in Beginning of First Grade

Measure	Performance	Descriptor
DIBELS Letter Naming Fluency	LNF < 25	At Risk
	25 <= LNF < 37	Some Risk
	LNF >= 37	Low Risk
DIBELS Phoneme Segmentation Fluency	PSF < 10	Deficit
	10 <= PSF < 35	Emerging
	PSF >= 35	Established
DIBELS Nonsense Word Fluency	NWF < 13	At Risk
	13 <= NWF < 24	Some Risk
	NWF >= 24	Low Risk

Table 8

Instructional Recommendations for Individual Patterns of Performance on Beginning of First Grade DIBELS Benchmark Assessment

Letter Naming Fluency	Phoneme Segmentation Fluency	Nonsense Word Fluency	Percent Meeting Later Goals				Incidence	Instructional Support Recommendation
			Middle 1		End 1			
			Pctile	NWF	ORF	Average		
At Risk	Deficit	At Risk	3	6	13	10	More Common	Intensive - Needs Substantial Intervention
At Risk	Emerging	At Risk	8	10	18	14	More Common	Intensive - Needs Substantial Intervention
At Risk	Established	At Risk	11	11	20	16	Unusual	Intensive - Needs Substantial Intervention
At Risk	Deficit	Some Risk	12	15	27	21	Unusual	Intensive - Needs Substantial Intervention
Some Risk	Deficit	At Risk	13	12	31	21	Unusual	Intensive - Needs Substantial Intervention
At Risk	Emerging	Some Risk	15	20	32	26	More Common	Strategic - Additional Intervention
Some Risk	Emerging	At Risk	17	18	37	27	Unusual	Strategic - Additional Intervention
Some Risk	Established	At Risk	19	20	35	28	Unusual	Strategic - Additional Intervention
At Risk	Established	Some Risk	20	25	32	28	Unusual	Strategic - Additional Intervention
Low Risk	Deficit	At Risk	21	22	46	34	Extremely Rare	Strategic - Additional Intervention
Some Risk	Deficit	Some Risk	22	21	47	34	Unusual	Strategic - Additional Intervention
Some Risk	Emerging	Some Risk	24	26	47	37	More Common	Strategic - Additional Intervention
At Risk	Deficit	Low Risk	26	30	45	37	Extremely Rare	Strategic - Additional Intervention
Some Risk	Established	Some Risk	28	29	49	39	More Common	Strategic - Additional Intervention
Low Risk	Emerging	At Risk	30	29	57	43	Unusual	Strategic - Additional Intervention
Low Risk	Established	At Risk	31	33	59	46	Extremely Rare	Strategic - Additional Intervention
At Risk	Emerging	Low Risk	31	40	54	47	Extremely Rare	Strategic - Additional Intervention
Some Risk	Deficit	Low Risk	32	37	61	49	Extremely Rare	Strategic - Additional Intervention
At Risk	Established	Low Risk	33	43	56	49	Unusual	Strategic - Additional Intervention
Low Risk	Deficit	Some Risk	34	35	66	50	Unusual	Strategic - Additional Intervention
Low Risk	Emerging	Some Risk	36	36	72	54	More Common	Benchmark - At grade level
Low Risk	Established	Some Risk	40	41	71	56	More Common	Benchmark - At grade level
Some Risk	Emerging	Low Risk	44	46	68	57	More Common	Benchmark - At grade level
Some Risk	Established	Low Risk	47	51	66	59	More Common	Benchmark - At grade level
Low Risk	Deficit	Low Risk	51	51	76	64	Unusual	Benchmark - At grade level
Low Risk	Emerging	Low Risk	56	66	86	76	More Common	Benchmark - At grade level
Low Risk	Established	Low Risk	81	78	90	84	More Common	Benchmark - At grade level

Note: Percent meeting goal is the conditional percent of children who meet the end of first grade goal of 40 or more on DIBELS ORF. Based on *n* of approximately 32,000 students, 638 schools, and 255 school districts.

Middle of First Grade Instructional Recommendation

In the middle of first grade, the cut scores for established skills and risk status are summarized in Table 9. The instructional recommendations corresponding to patterns of performance in the middle of first grade are summarized in Table 10. The benchmark goal for the middle of first grade is a score of 50 or more on the NWF measure. For the most part, it is extremely rare for a student to have established skills on NWF and less than established skills on PSF. In addition to established skills on NWF, it also appears important that students are beginning to apply those skills in connected text reading at least 20 correct words per minute on the ORF measure. For students with established skills on NWF and who are reading at least 20 words correct per minute, the odds of achieving the first grade reading outcomes are 97 to 100 percent. However, even if students have established skills on PSF and NWF, if they are reading fewer than 20 words correct per minute, their odds of achieving the first grade reading goal fall to 24 to 49 percent (with an instructional recommendation of strategic support). Students with combined risk factors in NWF and ORF are likely to require intensive intervention to achieve first grade reading outcomes.

In the middle of first grade, the ordering of DIBELS performance patterns does not follow exactly the conditional percent achieving reading outcomes. In particular, 100 percent of students with a deficit on PSF, established on NWF, and low risk on ORF achieved the first grade reading goal. However, that pattern was extremely rare and we decided to rank it below the similar patterns with higher phonemic awareness skills. A similar change in ordering of patterns was done for emerging NWF and low risk on ORF.

Table 9

Descriptive Levels of Performance in Middle of First Grade

Measure	Performance	Descriptor
DIBELS Phoneme Segmentation Fluency	PSF < 10	Deficit
	10 <= PSF < 35	Emerging
	PSF >= 35	Established
DIBELS Nonsense Word Fluency	NWF < 30	Deficit
	30 <= NWF < 50	Emerging
	NWF >= 50	Established
DIBELS Oral Reading Fluency	ORF < 8	At Risk
	8 <= ORF < 20	Some Risk
	ORF >= 20	Low Risk

Table 10

Instructional Recommendations for Individual Patterns of Performance on Middle of First Grade DIBELS Benchmark Assessment

Phoneme Segmentation Fluency	Nonsense Word Fluency	DIBELS Oral Reading Fluency	Percentile	Percent Meeting End ORF Goal	Incidence	Instructional Support Recommendation
Deficit	Deficit	At Risk	1	1	Unusual	Intensive - Needs Substantial Intervention
Emerging	Deficit	At Risk	3	2	More Common	Intensive - Needs Substantial Intervention
Established	Deficit	At Risk	6	2	More Common	Intensive - Needs Substantial Intervention
Deficit	Emerging	At Risk	8	4	Extremely Rare	Intensive - Needs Substantial Intervention
Emerging	Emerging	At Risk	8	7	Unusual	Intensive - Needs Substantial Intervention
Established	Emerging	At Risk	10	8	More Common	Intensive - Needs Substantial Intervention
Deficit	Established	Some Risk	12	14	Extremely Rare	Intensive - Needs Substantial Intervention
Emerging	Deficit	Some Risk	13	17	More Common	Intensive - Needs Substantial Intervention
Established	Deficit	Some Risk	15	18	More Common	Intensive - Needs Substantial Intervention
Deficit	Established	At Risk	17	20	Extremely Rare	Strategic - Additional Intervention
Emerging	Established	At Risk	17	23	Extremely Rare	Strategic - Additional Intervention
Established	Established	At Risk	17	24	Extremely Rare	Strategic - Additional Intervention
Deficit	Emerging	Some Risk	17	28	Extremely Rare	Strategic - Additional Intervention
Emerging	Emerging	Some Risk	19	29	More Common	Strategic - Additional Intervention
Established	Emerging	Some Risk	26	30	More Common	Strategic - Additional Intervention
Deficit	Established	Some Risk	32	31	Extremely Rare	Strategic - Additional Intervention
Emerging	Established	Some Risk	32	42	Extremely Rare	Strategic - Additional Intervention
Established	Established	Some Risk	35	49	More Common	Strategic - Additional Intervention
Deficit	Emerging	Low Risk	38	73	Extremely Rare	Strategic - Additional Intervention
Deficit	Deficit	Low Risk	38	79	Extremely Rare	Strategic - Additional Intervention
Emerging	Deficit	Low Risk	38	73	Extremely Rare	Strategic - Additional Intervention
Established	Deficit	Low Risk	39	74	Unusual	Strategic - Additional Intervention
Emerging	Emerging	Low Risk	42	87	More Common	Benchmark - At grade level
Established	Emerging	Low Risk	49	86	More Common	Benchmark - At grade level
Deficit	Established	Low Risk	56	100	Extremely Rare	Benchmark - At grade level
Emerging	Established	Low Risk	58	97	More Common	Benchmark - At grade level
Established	Established	Low Risk	80	97	More Common	Benchmark - At grade level

Note: Percent meeting goal is the conditional percent of children who meet the end of first grade goal of 40 or more on DIBELS ORF. Based on $n = 34,794$ students, 666 schools, 266 school districts.

End of First Grade Instructional Recommendation

At the end of first grade, instructional recommendations are based directly on ORF reading level. Students who meet the ORF goal of 40 or more words correct per minute are likely to have established PSF and NWF skills as well. Reading 40 or more words correct per minute and displaying a deficit in either PSF or NWF is an extremely rare pattern, and indicates a need to retest the students' skills on PSF and NWF if there is any concern about their performance. Students who meet the end of first grade benchmark goal on ORF have odds of 75 to 92 percent of achieving the second grade goal for more common patterns of performance. Students who are reading below 20 words correct per minute at the end of first grade are at risk for reading difficulty in second grade with odds of 10 to 18 percent of achieving the second grade reading goal for more common patterns. For students reading less than 20 words correct at the end of first grade, substantial, intensive instructional intervention is recommended.

Table 11

Descriptive Levels of Performance in End of First Grade

Measure	Performance	Descriptor
DIBELS Phoneme Segmentation Fluency	PSF < 10	Deficit
	10 <= PSF < 35	Emerging
	PSF >= 35	Established
DIBELS Nonsense Word Fluency	NWF < 30	Deficit
	30 <= NWF < 50	Emerging
	NWF >= 50	Established
DIBELS Oral Reading Fluency	ORF < 20	At Risk
	20 <= ORF < 40	Some Risk
	ORF >= 40	Low Risk

Table 12

Instructional Recommendations for Individual Patterns of Performance on End of First Grade DIBELS Benchmark Assessment

Phoneme Segmentation Fluency	Nonsense Word Fluency	DIBELS Oral Reading Fluency	Percentile	Percent Meeting End Second Goal	Incidence	Instructional Support Recommendation
Deficit	Deficit	At Risk	0	4	Extremely Rare	Intensive - Needs Substantial Intervention
Emerging	Deficit	At Risk	1	3	Unusual	Intensive - Needs Substantial Intervention
Established	Deficit	At Risk	2	5	Unusual	Intensive - Needs Substantial Intervention
Deficit	Emerging	At Risk	3	0	Extremely Rare	Intensive - Needs Substantial Intervention
Emerging	Emerging	At Risk	4	8	Unusual	Intensive - Needs Substantial Intervention
Established	Emerging	At Risk	7	10	More Common	Intensive - Needs Substantial Intervention
Deficit	Established	At Risk	9	0	Extremely Rare	Intensive - Needs Substantial Intervention
Emerging	Established	At Risk	9	24	Extremely Rare	Intensive - Needs Substantial Intervention
Established	Established	At Risk	11	18	More Common	Intensive - Needs Substantial Intervention
Deficit	Deficit	Some Risk	12	0	Extremely Rare	Strategic - Additional Intervention
Emerging	Deficit	Some Risk	13	35	Extremely Rare	Strategic - Additional Intervention
Established	Deficit	Some Risk	13	20	Extremely Rare	Strategic - Additional Intervention
Deficit	Emerging	Some Risk	14	0	Extremely Rare	Strategic - Additional Intervention
Emerging	Emerging	Some Risk	14	36	Unusual	Strategic - Additional Intervention
Established	Emerging	Some Risk	18	31	More Common	Strategic - Additional Intervention
Deficit	Established	Some Risk	21	0	Extremely Rare	Strategic - Additional Intervention
Emerging	Established	Some Risk	22	48	Unusual	Strategic - Additional Intervention
Established	Established	Some Risk	28	47	More Common	Strategic - Additional Intervention
Deficit	Deficit	Low Risk	35	100	Extremely Rare	Benchmark - At grade level
Emerging	Deficit	Low Risk	35	65	Extremely Rare	Benchmark - At grade level
Established	Deficit	Low Risk	35	65	Extremely Rare	Benchmark - At grade level
Deficit	Emerging	Low Risk	35	0	Extremely Rare	Benchmark - At grade level
Emerging	Emerging	Low Risk	36	86	Unusual	Benchmark - At grade level
Established	Emerging	Low Risk	39	75	More Common	Benchmark - At grade level
Deficit	Established	Low Risk	42	75	Extremely Rare	Benchmark - At grade level
Emerging	Established	Low Risk	44	92	More Common	Benchmark - At grade level
Established	Established	Low Risk	74	92	More Common	Benchmark - At grade level

Note: Percent meeting goal is the conditional percent of children who meet the end of second grade goal of 90 or more on DIBELS ORF. Based on n = 6,239 students, 64 participating districts, and 137 participating schools.

Beginning Second Grade Instructional Recommendation

The recommended beginning of second grade cut scores for low risk and at risk are reported in Table 13 along with the accompanying instructional recommendation. The beginning of second grade cut scores are not directly comparable to the end of first grade cutoffs. Both the at-risk score and the low-risk score are higher at the beginning of second grade. In part, the higher scores are due to the need for continual growth in reading skills in order for a student to be on track for successful reading outcomes. The end of first grade encompasses the final three months of first grade. The beginning of second grade includes the first three months of second grade. Students should be making continual progress over that span of time. The higher cut scores are also due to more rigorous cutoffs. At the end of first grade, the cutoffs of 20 and 40 correspond to the 13th and 35th percentiles, respectively. In the beginning of second grade, the cutoffs of 26 and 44 correspond to the 20th and 40th percentiles, respectively. However, the odds of achieving second grade reading goals are similar for students with an intensive instructional recommendation: 6 percent at end of first grade, 10 percent in beginning of second. The odds are also similar for students with a benchmark instructional recommendation: 90 percent at end of first grade, 89 percent in the beginning of second grade. The odds of achieving subsequent benchmark goals were the primary consideration in establishing cut scores.

Table 13

Descriptive Levels of Performance in Beginning of Second Grade

Performance	Descriptor	Conditional Percent Reading 90 or More on End of Second Grade DIBELS ORF	Instructional Recommendation
ORF < 26	At Risk	6%	Intensive - Needs Substantial Intervention
26 <= ORF < 44	Some Risk	35%	Strategic - Additional Intervention
ORF >= 44	Low Risk	89%	Benchmark - At Grade Level

Note: Based on *n* = 13,612 students, 107 participating districts, and 262 participating schools.

Middle of Second Grade Instructional Recommendation

The cut scores for levels of risk and corresponding instructional recommendations for the middle of second grade are reported in Table 14. A consistent pattern emerges in second and later grades. When students are on track for successful reading outcomes (i.e., at benchmark or low-risk status), the odds are strongly in favor of achieving subsequent goals (about 90 percent) as intended with the decision rules. The odds are strongly against achieving subsequent goals (less than 10 percent unless they receive very intensive intervention) for students identified as at risk or as needing intensive intervention. Both of these odds are consistent with the primary consideration in establishing cutoffs for DIBELS Benchmark Assessment. However, for the strategic instructional recommendation, the intent was for the odds to be about 50-50 of achieving subsequent literacy goals, as obtained for earlier grade levels. Beginning at about the end of first grade, the odds of achieving subsequent goals for students identified as needing strategic instructional support fall increasingly below 50 percent.

Table 14

Descriptive Levels of Performance in Middle of Second Grade

Performance	Descriptor	Percent Achieving Third Grade Goal	Instructional Recommendation
ORF < 52	At Risk	8%	Intensive - Needs Substantial Intervention
52 <= ORF < 68	Some Risk	38%	Strategic - Additional Intervention
ORF >= 68	Low Risk	90%	Benchmark - At Grade Level

Note: Based on *n* = 15,806 students, 120 participating districts, and 299 participating schools.

End of Second Grade Instructional Recommendation

The cut scores for levels of risk and corresponding instructional recommendations for the end of second grade are reported in Table 15. At the end of second grade, the crucial outcome is end of third grade reading skills. With each subsequent grade, the predictive utility becomes stronger—meaning that we can have more confidence in our decisions but also meaning that it becomes increasingly difficult to thwart the predictions of reading success or difficulty.

Table 15

Descriptive Levels of Performance in End of Second Grade

Performance	Descriptor	Percent Achieving Third Grade Goal	Instructional Recommendation
ORF < 70	At Risk	7%	Intensive - Needs Substantial Intervention
70 <= ORF < 90	Some Risk	34%	Strategic - Additional Intervention
ORF >= 90	Low Risk	89%	Benchmark - At Grade Level

Note: Based on *n* = 3,758 students, 31 participating districts, and 79 participating schools.

Beginning of Third Grade Instructional Recommendation

The cut scores for levels of risk and corresponding instructional recommendations for the beginning of third grade are reported in Table 16. For students identified as at risk at the beginning of third grade, about 20 percent from the system-wide percentile ranks (Good et al., 2002), the odds of achieving the end of third grade reading outcome are of serious concern. For students identified as low risk with a benchmark instructional recommendation, about 60 percent based on the system-wide percentile ranks, the odds of achieving the end of third grade reading outcome are strongly in their favor.

Table 16

Descriptive Levels of Performance in Beginning of Third Grade

Performance	Descriptor	Percent Achieving Third Grade Goal	Instructional Recommendation
ORF < 53	At Risk	3%	Intensive - Needs Substantial Intervention
53 <= ORF < 77	Some Risk	34%	Strategic - Additional Intervention
ORF >= 77	Low Risk	90%	Benchmark - At Grade Level

Note: Based on *n* = 9,662 students, 78 participating districts, and 180 participating schools.

Middle of Third Grade Instructional Recommendation

The cut scores for levels of risk and corresponding instructional recommendations for the middle of third grade are reported in Table 17. The cut scores again correspond to the 20th and 40th percentile based on the system-wide percentile ranks (Good et al., 2002).

Table 17

Descriptive Levels of Performance in the Middle of Third Grade

Performance	Descriptor	Percent Achieving Third Grade Goal	Instructional Recommendation
ORF < 67	At Risk	3%	Intensive - Needs Substantial Intervention
67 <= ORF < 92	Some Risk	27%	Strategic - Additional Intervention
ORF >= 92	Low Risk	90%	Benchmark - At Grade Level

Note: Based on *n* = 11,811 students, 91 participating districts, and 219 participating schools.

End of Third Grade Instructional Recommendation

The cut scores for levels of risk and corresponding instructional recommendations for the end of third grade are reported in Table 18. The cut scores correspond to the 16th and 40th percentile based on the system-wide percentile ranks (Good et al., 2002). In Table 18, the odds of achieving subsequent reading goals are represented by a question mark because the most important and meaningful literacy outcome is likely to vary from state to state. For example, Good, Simmons, & Kame'enui (2001) reported that the odds of receiving a rating of "meets expectations" or "exceeds expectations" on the Oregon Statewide Assessment Test were 96 percent if students scored in the low risk or benchmark range on the ORF at the end of third grade. Sibley, Biwer, & Hesch (2001) reported that the odds of meeting or exceeding standards on the Illinois State Assessment Test were 99 percent for students scoring in the low risk or benchmark range on the end of third grade DIBELS Benchmark Assessment. Similar results were found by Linner (2001, January).

The DIBELS Data System has the capability to include an external outcome measure that can be used to evaluate the predictive utility of the ORF. Each state assessment should be examined in this way by users of the DIBELS Benchmark Assessment to evaluate the predictive utility of the measures for their state context.

Table 18

Descriptive Levels of Performance in the End of Third Grade

Performance	Descriptor	Percent Achieving Subsequent Reading Goal	Instructional Recommendation
ORF < 80	At Risk	?	Intensive - Needs Substantial Intervention
80 <= ORF < 110	Some Risk	?	Strategic - Additional Intervention
ORF >= 110	Low Risk	?	Benchmark - At Grade Level

Discussion

This technical report is intended to make public the decision rules used in the DIBELS Data System and to summarize evidence on the predictive utility of the DIBELS cutoffs both as indicators of risk and as instructional goals. At any point in time, students who are at risk have the odds seriously against achieving subsequent early literacy goals—unless they are provided with substantial, sustained, intensive intervention support. But, even more important, for students prior to that point in time, the benchmark goal represents an instructional target that will establish the odds in favor of achieving subsequent early literacy goals.

References

American Federation of Teachers. (1999). *Teaching reading is rocket science*. Washington, DC: AFT.

Armbruster, B., Lehr, F., & Osborn, J. (2001). *Put reading first: The research building blocks for teaching children to read, kindergarten through grade 3*. Washington, DC: National Institute for Literacy.

Children's Educational Services. (1987a). *Test of oral reading fluency*. Eden Prairie, MN: Children's Educational Services.

Children's Educational Services. (1987b). *Test of reading fluency.* Minneapolis, MN: Children's Educational Services.

Good, R. H., Gruba, J., & Kaminski, R. A. (2001). Best practices in using Dynamic Indicators of Basic Early Literacy Skills (DIBELS) in an outcomes-driven model. In A. Thomas & J. Grimes (Eds.), *Best Practices in School Psychology IV* (p. 679–700). Washington, DC: National Association of School Psychologists.

Good, R. H., & Jefferson, G. (1998). Contemporary perspectives on curriculum-based measurement validity. In M. R. Shinn (Ed.), *Advanced Applications of Curriculum-Based Measurement* (pp. 61–88). New York: Guilford.

Good, R. H., & Kaminski, R. A. (Eds.). (2002). *Dynamic indicators of basic early literacy skills* (6th ed.). Eugene, OR: Institute for Development of Educational Achievement.

Good, R. H., Kaminski, R. A., & Dill, S. (2002). DIBELS oral reading fluency. In R. H. Good & R. A. Kaminski (Eds.), *Dynamic Indicators of Basic Early Literacy Skills* (6th ed.). Eugene, OR: Institute for the Development of Educational Achievement. Available: http://dibels.uoregon.edu/.

Good, R. H., Kaminski, R. A., Shinn, M., Bratten, J., Shinn, M., & Laimon, L. (2002). *Technical adequacy and decision-making utility of DIBELS.* (Technical Report in Preparation). Eugene: University of Oregon.

Good, R. H., Kaminski, R. A., Shinn, M., Bratten, J., Shinn, M., & Laimon, L. (in press). *Technical adequacy and decision making utility of DIBELS* (Technical Report). Eugene: University of Oregon.

Good, R. H., Kaminski, R. A., Simmons, D., & Kame'enui, E. J. (2001). Using dynamic indicators of basic early literacy skills (DIBELS) in an outcomes-driven model. *OSSC Bulletin, 44*(1), 1–24.

Good, R. H., Simmons, D. C., & Kame'enui, E. J. (2001). The importance and decision-making utility of a continuum of fluency-based indicators of foundational reading skills for third-grade high-stakes outcomes. *Scientific Studies of Reading*, 5, 257–288.

Good, R. H., Simmons, D. C., & Smith, S. (1998). Effective academic interventions in the United States: Evaluating and enhancing the acquisition of early reading skills. *School Psychology Review, 27,* 45–56.

Good, R. H., Wallin, J., Simmons, D. C., Kame'enui, E. J., & Kaminski, R. A. (2002). *System-wide percentile ranks for DIBELS benchmark assessment* (Technical Report No. 9). Eugene: University of Oregon.

Kaminski, R. A., & Good, R. H. (1992). *Dynamic indicators of basic early literacy skills (DIBELS) phoneme segmentation fluency.* (Unpublished Measure). Eugene: University of Oregon.

Kaminski, R. A., & Good, R. H. (1996). Toward a technology for assessing basic early literacy skills. *School Psychology Review, 25,* 215–227.

Kaminski, R. A., & Good, R. H. (1998). Assessing early literacy skills in a problem-solving model: Dynamic Indicators of Basic Early Literacy Skills. In M. R. Shinn (Ed.), *Advanced Applications of Curriculum-Based Measurement* (pp. 113–142). New York: Guilford.

Laimon, D. E. (1994). *The effects of a home-based and center-based intervention on at-risk preschool children's early literacy skills.* Unpublished doctoral dissertation, University of Oregon, Eugene.

Laimon, D. E., & Good, R. H. (1994). *Dynamic indicators of basic early literacy skills (DIBELS) onset recognition fluency.* (Unpublished Measure). Eugene: University of Oregon.

Learning First Alliance. (2000). *Every child reading: A professional development guide.* Washington, DC: Learning First Alliance.

Linner, S. (2001, January). *Curriculum-based assessment in reading used as a predictor for the Alaska benchmark test.* Paper presented at the Alaska Special Education Conference, Anchorage, AK.

Marston, D., & Magnusson, D. (1988). Curriculum-based measurement: District level implementation. In J. Graden, J. Zins, & M. Curtis (Eds.), *Alternative Educational Delivery Systems: Enhancing Instructional Options for All Students* (pp. 137–172). Washington, DC: National Association of School Psychology.

National Reading Panel. (2000a). *Report of the National Reading Panel: Teaching children to read, an evidence-based assessment of the scientific research literature on reading and its implications for reading instruction.* Washington, DC: National Institute for Child Health and Human Development.

National Reading Panel. (2000b). *Teaching children to read: An evidence-based assessment of the scientific research literature on reading and its implications for reading instruction.* Bethesda, MD: National Institute of Child Health and Human Development. Available: http://www.nationalreadingpanel.org/.

Nova Development Corporation. (1998). *Art explosion.* Calabasas, CA: Author.

Nunnally, J. C. (1978). *Psychometric theory* (2nd ed.). New York: McGraw-Hill.

Public Law 107–110, 107th Cong., 1st sess. (3 January 2001), *No Child Left Behind Act of 2001.*

Rayner, K., Foorman, B. R., Perfetti, C. A., Pesetsky, D., & Seidenberg, M. S. (2001). How psychological science informs the teaching of reading. *Psychological Science, 2,* 31–74.

Reading Excellence Act. (1999). [on-line] Available: http://www.ed.gov/offices/OESE/REA/legis.html.

Salvia, J., & Ysseldyke, J. E. (2001). *Assessment* (8th ed.). Boston: Houghton Mifflin.

Shinn, M. R. (1995). Best practices in curriculum-based measurement and its use in a problem-solving model. In A. Thomas & J. Grimes (Eds.), *Best Practices in School Psychology III* (pp. 547–567). Washington, DC: National Association of School Psychologists.

Shinn, M. R. (Ed.). (1989). *Curriculum-based measurement: Assessing special children.* New York: Guilford.

Sibley, D., Biwer, D., & Hesch, A. (2001). *Unpublished data.* Arlington Heights, IL: Arlington Heights School District 25.

Simmons, D. C., & Kame'enui, E. J. (Eds.) (1998). *What reading research tells us about children with diverse learning needs: Bases and basics.* Mahwah, NJ: Erlbaum.

Snow, C., Burns, S., and Griffin, P. (1998). *Preventing reading difficulty in young children.* Washington, DC: National Research Council, National Academy of Sciences Press.

Tindal, G., Marston, D., & Deno, S.L. (1983). *The reliability of direct and repeated measurement.* (Research Report 109). Minneapolis: University of Minnesota Institute for Research on Learning Disabilities.

Torgesen, J. K., Alexander, A. W., Wagner, R. K., Rashotte, C. A., Voeller, K., Conway, T., & Rose, E. (2001). Intensive remedial instruction for children with severe reading disabilities: Immediate and long-term outcomes from two instructional approaches. *Journal of Learning Disabilities, 34,* 33–58.

Zigler, E., & Styfco, S. J. (1994). Head start: Criticisms in a constructive context. *American Psychologist, 49,* 127–132.